CANNON
⸎BEACH⸎

Watercolor painting of Cannon Beach
from Ecola State Park by Evelyn Hicks

CANNON ~BEACH~

A Place By The Sea

By Terence O'Donnell

CANNON BEACH HISTORICAL SOCIETY

OREGON HISTORICAL SOCIETY PRESS

Library of Congress Cataloging-in-Publication Data

O'Donnell, Terence.
    Cannon Beach: a place by the sea /by Terence O'Donnell
      p. cm.
    Includes bibliographical referneces and index.
    ISBN 0-87595-260-7 (alk. paper)
    1. Cannon Beach (Or.)—History. I. Cannon Beach Historical
Society. II. title.
F884.C23036 1996
979.5'46—dc20   95-47304
                                            CIP

First edition

Designed and produced by the Oregon Historical Society Press.

The paper used in this publication meets the minimum requirements of
American National Standard for Information Sciences—Permanence of
Paper for Printed Library Materials, ANSI Z39.48-1984.

Printed in the United States of America.
Oregon Historical Society Press
1200 SW Park
Portland, Oregon 97205-2483

Red st

pnw
979.54
od 2.1

Roberts   14 95   3-6-97

*For Maurie and Mary Clark, without
whose generosity this book could not have
been published and for the late Jim Dennon,
without whose research it could not
have been written*

A RED STOCKING BOOK

1997

CONTENTS

*From this point I beheld
the grandest and most pleasing prospect
which my eyes ever surveyed.*

CAPTAIN WILLIAM CLARK,
JANUARY 1806

ACKNOWLEDGEMENTS

As NOTED IN THE DEDICATION, this book could not have been published without the generosity of Maurie and Mary Clark nor could it have been written without the research done by the late Jim Dennon. The author is profoundly grateful.

Providing encouragement and knowledge were the past and present members of the Cannon Beach Historical Society: Karolyn Adamson, Roland Burrows, Frank and Eleanor Chown, David and Alma English, Roger Evanson, William Gittelsohn, Katy Grant-Hanson, Treva Haskell, Marlene Laws, Barbara Levine, Sally Little,

Margaret McCluskey, Kent Price, Dan and Molly Schausten, Barbara and Herbert Schwab, George Shields, Ann Smeaton, Travis and Irene Tyrrell, and Ann Wierum. Of these board members, three were of particular assistance: Barbara Schwab, the liaison between the author and the board, gave many hours to the host of issues and problems related to the research, writing, and publication of the book; George Shields provided much useful information on the history of Cannon Beach; and Ann Wierun on several occasions took time to open History House to the author and help him with his research while he was there.

Taped interviews conducted by the Seaside chapter of the American Association of University Women, and by Jim Dennon, David Pastor, William Gittelsohn, Barbara and Herbert Schwab, and George Shields, provided the author with much crucial information. Though all the interviews were informative, those from which specific information was taken included the interviews given by Edward and Erna Carlson, Maurie Clark, Ken Cole, Paul Bartels, Elaine Dennon, Heather Goodenough, Lucille Houston, Juanita Mahon Kincaid, Kenneth Kraemer, Marie Marshall, Mae McCoy, Harold McKay, Gainor Minott, Theodore Nickelsen, Alvena Nyberg, Les and Hatti Ordway, Don Osborne, Sr., Marion Pattullo, Kent and Florence Price, Janet Rekate, George Shields, Margaret Sroufe, Herbert Schwab, Bridget Snow, William Steidel, Tom Turner, and John Yeon. These interviews and many others are on file at the Cannon Beach Historical Society.

Other persons helpful to the the author's research were Dr. John Eliot Allen, Rainmar Bartl, Herbert Beals, Elise Osburn Blisset, Paul Brinkman, John Buckley, Bud George, John Griffin, Bruce Hamilton, Dolly Hutchinson, Ken Kraemer, Peter Lindsey, Tim Lindsey, Millard McClung, Mary Ann Oyala, Elizabeth Potter, Steve Prince, Harry Teller, Violet Thompson, Ray Watkins, Helen Westbrook, and John Williams. Special thanks as well to Elaine Dennon, Jim Dennon's mother, who provided all her son's records, files, and tapes to the Cannon Beach Historical Society and likewise

Jessica Bartels Palfreyman who gave tapes of interviews of her father, Paul Bartels to the Society. Barbara Levine and Ann Smeaton were most enterprising in finding many good photographs for the book. David and Alma English's *Arch Cape Chronicles*, provided information on that community.

Finally, the author is most grateful to the several organizations which contributed to the book, most importantly to the Oregon Historical Society. Adair Law, the managing editor of the Oregon Historical Society Press, quietly and gracefully guided the manuscript through to publication. I am most grateful as well to the text editor, Nancy Trotic; the designer, Barbara Osborne; the cover illustrator, Evelyn Hicks; Susan Seyl and Evan Schneider for their assistance with the photographs, and finally Chet Orloff, the director of the Society, for his overall support of the project. Other organizations which provided generous help were the Clatsop County Historical Society and Heritage Museum, the Seaside Museum and Historical Society, the Tillamook County Historical Society and Museum, The Colulmbia River Maritime Museum, the Cannon Beach Chamber of Commerce, and the Cannon Beach Library.

The author's gratitude to all.

INTRODUCTION

THERE WAS NO SEASHORE IN THE GARDEN OF EDEN. Indeed, through most of human history the seashore has been feared as a place of danger to be avoided. Mountains might have their wild animals and freezing snows, their avalanches and crevasses, the forests even wilder animals as well as goblins and witches. But neither could match the terror inspired by the sea and its shore.

For good reason. There was, for example, the sea's deceptiveness, its capriciousness. Serene as a millpond on a summer's day, it could suddenly leap with fury, flinging ships and men against the rocks or pitching them down into Davy Jones's locker. There were its attacks on the land, grinding it down, breaking it up, submerging it beneath great tidal waves. Feared, too, were the monsters of the deep—that sea dragon pictured in the corner of old maps, the octopus, the shark, and that great leviathan famed for gobbling up poor Jonah. Then, something by no means minor, that sickness of the sea, the dreaded *mal de mer*, which from the beginning of time has driven its victims to pray for death. Finally, it was the sea that served as the instrument of God's wrath at the sinfulness of man, the Flood, turning the whole world into an ocean. At least so far as the distant past is concerned, the sea's reputation was not the best.

Scholars disagree, but some argue that a favorable view of the sea began in the seventeenth century and through the agency of that remarkable people, the Dutch. In part, it is said, this came from the fact that the Dutch tamed—or anyway partially tamed—the sea in two respects. In their exceptionally seaworthy ships, they roamed the seas to an even greater extent than those earlier seafaring peoples, the Phoenicians, Vikings, and Arabs. The trade these ships engaged in brought great riches to the Dutch, and that naturally predisposed them to look with favor on the medium that literally supported their trade. Secondly, the Dutch successfully defied the sea by diking their land, the sea at last at bay.

Another element in this changed attitude toward the sea came not from trade or engineering but from art. Painters, by their choice of subject, have often determined our taste in scenery. In Holland, where the sea was not only omnipresent but beneficent in the riches it bestowed, painters, palette in hand, turned to it. The result was that people began to see the sea as it had never been seen before—as beautiful.

It was not much more than a century or so later that three other developments came along that further enhanced our view of the sea and its shore. One was the movement called Romanticism, which took as one of its landscape ideals not the sun-filled and sheltered pastoral valley but the dark and storm-fraught coast.

The second development was the belief that sea water and sea air were therapeutic. In the eighteenth century and down into the nineteenth, this belief in the sea's curative properties became at times a mania. People drank sea water for gout, for worms, and as a laxative. They bathed in sea water for hypochondria, sterility, and nymphomania. And they breathed in the sea air for everything. Though faith in these particular cures has passed, there is still the notion about that sea air is healthful by virtue of its ions; and, until the increase in skin cancers, sunbathing at the coast was considered a protection against the ills of winter.

The third development to draw people to the shore was the nineteenth-century industrialization of the cities, which in its first phases befouled urban centers with smoke, dirt, stench, and racket. Those who had the time and money fled to the fresh and cleansing breezes of the shore and the soothing lap of the waves.

꒤

The idea that the seashore was a place of beauty (and particularly of romantic beauty), the belief in its curative powers, and finally the shore as an escape from "the dark, Satanic mills" of early industrialization—all these finally led to that relatively new kind of community, the seaside resort.

The location of these resorts has always depended on transportation. Early resorts, before the time of railroads and automobiles, ordinarily developed in places that could be reached by water. On the Northwest coast, for example, Seaview, Washington, and Seaside, Oregon, were the first resorts of any note because they were near the Columbia River. Vacationers traveling by riverboat from Portland and other inland cities were put ashore at Ilwaco on the Washington side or Astoria on the Oregon side and then proceeded relatively short distances by wagon to their destination.

Next came the railroad, in 1889 to Seaview and the Long Beach Peninsula, in 1890 to Gearhart and Seaside. Thus was the wagon ride from the ports eliminated and access to these resorts greatly facilitated.

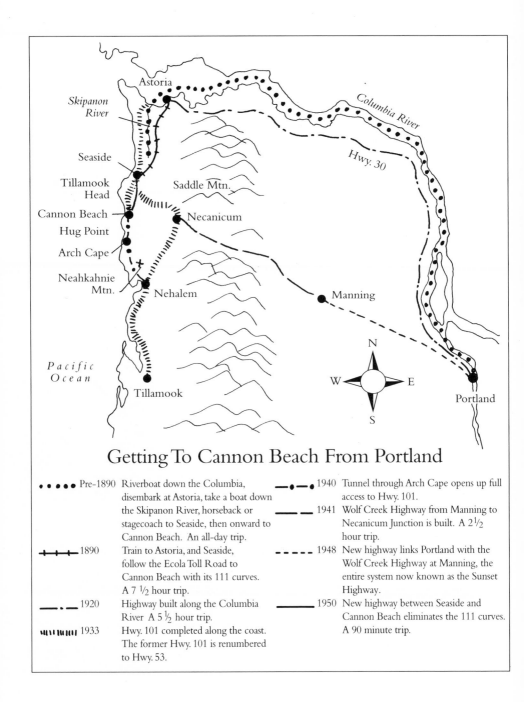

Getting To Cannon Beach From Portland

• • • • Pre-1890 Riverboat down the Columbia, disembark at Astoria, take a boat down the Skipanon River, horseback or stagecoach to Seaside, then onward to Cannon Beach. An all-day trip.

+ + + 1890 Train to Astoria, and Seaside, follow the Ecola Toll Road to Cannon Beach with its 111 curves. A 7 1/2 hour trip.

— · — 1920 Highway built along the Columbia River A 5 1/2 hour trip.

⊔⊔⊔⊔⊔⊔⊔ 1933 Hwy. 101 completed along the coast. The former Hwy. 101 is renumbered to Hwy. 53.

— · — · 1940 Tunnel through Arch Cape opens up full access to Hwy. 101.

——— 1941 Wolf Creek Highway from Manning to Necanicum Junction is built. A 2 1/2 hour trip.

- - - - 1948 New highway links Portland with the Wolf Creek Highway at Manning, the entire system now known as the Sunset Highway.

——— 1950 New highway between Seaside and Cannon Beach eliminates the 111 curves. A 90 minute trip.

Finally, the automobile. Automobiles reached the Northwest at the beginning of the century, but it was not until the 1930s that roads became sufficiently serviceable and automobiles sufficiently reliable that the latter came to have an impact on coastal places. Following World War II, that impact vastly increased and indeed to such a degree that some would call it a collision.

The automobile, unlike the water and the rails before it, did appreciably alter the character of seaside places. Now, ever more accessible, they grew in size; more importantly, and despite an increase in retirees at the coast, their population became largely transient. Previously, people commonly vacationed at the coast for weeks at a time, often staying the whole summer, and thus became a part of the community. There were a variety of reasons for these long-term stays, but one of the most important was that before the time of good cars and good roads, it took time and trouble to reach coastal resorts. It once was seven hours from Portland to the coast, on roads so winding that nausea was a condition of the trip. The travel time now being an hour and twenty minutes, most vacationers stay only a night or two or even just for the day. Another significant change is that now, with good roads and all-season accommodations, these coastal places are no longer "summer" resorts but resorts for winter as well.

Over the years, then, from their beginnings in the mid-nineteenth century, the character of seaside resorts has changed. On the other hand, there are certain constants. These appear to lie in the attraction the seacoast itself has had for certain kinds of people, as well as the particular effect the seacoast seems to have on almost any kind of person.

One type the coast has always attracted, at least since the time of the Romantic movement, has been those seeking self-knowledge, self-discovery, people who, to use the current phrase, are out to "find" themselves, to reassess their lives. It may be for this reason that so many "dropouts"—and not only in the 1960s and 70s but before and after as well—have ended up at coastal places. Why the sea and its shore should encourage such searchings is a mystery, but that it

*This 1888 photo shows the day's catch for a group of Portlanders
who had journeyed to North Beach, Washington.*

*Another group appropriately hatted, shod, corseted, and flounced takes
time to celebrate the day's outing with a photo.*

Walking on Cannon Beach seems incomplete without a dog in attendance.

Despite their coldness, wading in the waters of Cannon Beach is irresistible on a sunny day. The Tillamook Rock lighthouse can be seen on the left in the distance.

The sea air had a liberating influence on the limbs of both men and women. The gentlemen are from the Multnomah Athletic Club swimming team. The ladies are simply enjoying a fine day on the beach.

*With such a splendid backdrop, the Seaside Girl's Band of
Clatsop County stands to attention.*

*A fine day at the coast brings out the cars and even an airplane
in the far left corner of the photo.*

may do so can be attested to by almost anyone who has walked a deserted beach under the bowl of the sky and gazed out at the sea's infinity.

A related, curious and enduring effect of the seashore has been described by the travel essayist Jonathan Raban. "Legally, socially, morally the beach is a marginal zone to which marginal people tend to gravitate and where respectable folk tend to behave in marginal and eccentric ways." Raban's assertion that the coast draws "marginal people" brings to mind the friend who once opined that the whole of Oregon is slanted down to the west, with the result that all the kooks slide down to the coast! Despite the exaggeration, there is no doubt that seacoasts, including Oregon's, have always drawn the mildly eccentric—in the view of some, one of the pleasing features of coastal places.

As for Raban's other assertion, that respectable people at the seashore tend to behave in "marginal" ways, he goes on to characterize the coast as a place "where the social rules grow lax." Other writers, too (as well as police departments), have commented on what some would call the "liberating" influence of the seashore. Certainly, it is common experience that people at the seashore are wont to "let go," "unbend," "kick over the traces," and those other expressions indicating a lifting of inhibition. Yet somehow the sea air seems to gloss over—to redeem, as it were—whatever errancies may result. The process has been charmingly described by the American novelist Henry James, vacationing on the Riviera near the end of the last century. Observing a French actress bathing in the sea and reflecting on the suggestion of vice conveyed by her "liberated limbs" (except for the audacious ones, women's bathing costumes were still all-enveloping), James wrote: "There are some days here so still and radiant that it seems as if vice itself, steeped in such an air and in such a sea, might be diluted into innocence."

"Innocence." James is right, and perhaps in an even broader sense than he intends. For in general, when we think of the seashore, the association of innocence often hovers near. Why should the two be linked? One reason may lie in the memories of childhood summers so many have. The bucket, the spade, the sandcastle. Scampering into the wavelets, under the summer sun, holding tight to someone's hand. Eating marshmallows off the end of a stick in the light of a driftwood fire. A five-year-old I know, on seeing the beach for the first time, exclaimed: "Oh! What a big playground!" Indeed.

And not just for children, either, but for all of us is the seashore a kind of playground, a place to play—even, it would seem, for those who live there, so laid back are they. So perhaps this is the root of the association of seashore and innocence, for play by its very nature is innocent, even when a little errant.

And so, the seashore: the haunt of monsters, a scene for painters, a remedy pushed by the quacks, a refuge from the Satanic mills, an ashram for the discovery of self, a getaway for the libertine, and finally, for all of us, child or dotard, saint or sinner, a place to play in our different ways, here in these places by the sea—like Cannon Beach.

CHAPTER ONE

SOME TWO-THOUSAND YEARS AGO the Roman poet Ovid, in exile on the Black Sea coast, wrote to a friend in Rome that he had seen "land made from the sea and far from the ocean seashells lay and old anchors I have found here on the tops of mountains."

What Ovid wrote could be written of the Oregon coast as well, for where Cannon Beach now stands the ocean floor once lay. At some point during those watery millennia, the land mass of the continent began to move westward, gradually encroaching on the sea (as it continues to do today). Then in the Miocene epoch, twenty million years ago, the encroaching land cracked, spewing basaltic lava from its bowels over the ocean's mudstone floor. Next, there moved down from the polar regions great sheets of ice to glaciate the land for another million years. Finally, about twelve thousand years ago, the Ice Age ended, the last of the cataclysmic changes to occur. Thereafter it was only wind and fire, the rain, the surf, and the hand of man that would touch the place we see today: this nine-mile reach bracketed to the north by Tillamook Head, to the south by Silver Point; to the east by the coastal mountains, these sloping down to marine terraces of forest, swamp, and open meadow, crossed by Ecola Creek flowing from its origins at Onion Peak; then the beach, built up over centuries by sediment carried by the Columbia, lying now in crescents between the cliffed headlands, capes, and points, those diminished, basaltic spurs of the coastal mountains. And finally the sea, the sea with its offshore stacks, the *genius loci* of the place.

$\backsim$

This in general is what the first humans saw when they arrived at what is now called Cannon Beach. They had had a long journey. Beginning in Mongolia, they moved through the generations to Siberia, thence to Alaska, thereafter down the continent. About ten thousand years ago, they entered what is now called Oregon from the east, some moving ever farther west, finally to settle here on "the river with one bank," as they called the ocean.

Those who settled on the shore between Tillamook Head and the Siletz River were called the Tillamooks. They lived in small villages at the mouths of the coastal creeks, in houses built of cedar planks and peeled spruce roots. The interiors, lit by pitch torches and burning fish heads, were carpeted with ferns and rushes, a fire pit down the center, sleeping platforms to either side hung with mat partitions since two families often occupied one house. Here, in their capes of painted buckskin, they fed on what they took from land

2

Haystack Rock circa 1910.

Aerial view of Cannon Beach, circa 1930.

and sea—berries, game, salmon, shellfish. In these houses, too, their important rituals occurred: child naming and the ear piercing that accompanied it; the salmon ceremony to celebrate the spearing of the first steelhead of the season; and, most important of all, the winter dance in which their shaman received his power anew and by extension renewed the world as well. Food and shelter, their myths and rituals, these sustained them century after century, here between the river and the head.

The number of Tillamooks prior to the nineteenth century is unknown, but it is thought that in the 1780s they were infected by smallpox and their population was thus reduced. Lewis and Clark in 1805 and a Hudson's Bay Company census of 1838 estimated that they numbered about a thousand. By 1851, when the Tillamooks ceded their land to the United States, the official count was only two hundred. By the time of white settlement, at the end of the century, the villages of No-cost (at Cannon Beach) and Ma-ti (at Tolovana) no longer existed. Except for a few kitchen middens, or shell mounds, nothing of the Tillamooks remains—unless it be their ghosts.

෴

The root of those events that were to bring about the virtual extinction of the natives of the Oregon coast began its growth in the tall tales told by sailors in the dockside taverns of sixteenth-century Lisbon and Seville. Some of these tales concerned an area about which almost nothing was known: the northern reaches of that ocean that Magellan not long before had named the Pacific.

One tale told of a city called Fusang, founded by a Buddhist monk from Afghanistan! It was said to be located on a river two leagues wide in which there were fish the size of a horse and canoes of great size, too. The people of the place drank and ate out of jugs and bowls of gold. Even more astounding, their king had a tree hung with golden bells which, swinging in the air, would lull him to sleep!

The arches of Arch Cape.

An elk viewing Cannon Beach from Ecola State Park

Of particular interest, however, was that river two leagues wide (according to one definition of league, about the width of the Columbia at Astoria). And it was of interest because a great river ordinarily meant a deep river, which meant in turn that ocean-going ships might sail far inland to find not only gold but perhaps people to enslave, as well as to convert to the true faith. And so with these incentives, the search began for the fabled great river and its riches.

In 1543 an expedition under the command of Juan Cabrillo got as far as the Rogue River. But they found no Fusang there, nor, for that matter, any river two leagues wide. Other expeditions followed, but it was not until 1775, more than two hundred years later, that Bruno Heceta, sailing far north, came upon what he considered the telltale signs of a great river: seagulls in large numbers, muddy water, cross-currents, drifting logs. But Heceta and his crew were too weakened by scurvy to man a boat and cross the bar, and so were forced to sail away.

Three years later the great British maritime explorer Captain James Cook, searching for the river, passed it unknowingly on a stormy night. He was followed the same year, in 1778, by his countryman Captain John Meares. Meares deemed "the great river" no river at all, and so named its estuary Deception Bay and its northern promontory Cape Disappointment.

Meanwhile, the Americans had come to the Northwest coast. The first was Captain Robert Gray. Gray was not searching for the river at all but was engaged in trade: buttons and beads to the Indians in exchange for pelts to sell in China. It is commonly considered that it was Gray and his crew who in 1788 effected the first white contact with the Tillamooks—a tragic contact, as it turned out. While Gray's ship was anchored in what he was to call Murderers Bay (present-day Tillamook Bay), his black cabin boy was pursued by the Tillamooks, who, according to the ship's log, "drenched there knives and spears with savage feury in the boddy of the unfortunate youth."

In 1792 Gray returned to the Northwest coast, again on a trading voyage. In the same year, Captain George Vancouver was sent out by the British Admiralty to chart the coast and find the river. Passing the mouth, he, too, denied the evidence—that great fan of muddy water. But Captain Gray, arriving at the mouth a few weeks later, did not. And further, he had on a May morning of 1792 the greatest good luck: an exceptional convergence of currents, tide, and wind that permitted him to cross with safety one of the world's most treacherous bars. At long last, the great river so long sought had been found. Gray named it for his little ship, the *Columbia Rediviva*. The opening of what is now called Oregon had begun.

ᔕ

The news of Gray's discovery soon reached the ears of that most enquiring of men, the President of the Republic, Mr. Thomas Jefferson. Jefferson, curious to know how the Columbia might be reached overland, sent out his secretary, Captain Meriwether Lewis, and Lewis's friend, Captain William Clark, to plot a route. Traveling by way of the Missouri, overland, and by the Columbia itself, Lewis and Clark arrived at the mouth of the river in November of 1805 and there set up a winter camp they called Fort Clatsop after the local Indians. And a miserable winter it was, with fleas, rain, scant food, and much sickness. They were particularly depressed by the degraded condition of the Indians. In 1792 John Boit of Gray's crew had described the natives as "strait limb'd, fine looking fellows, and the women very pretty." Now, only fourteen years later, as a result of contact with the crews of the fur trading ships that had anchored in the Columbia following Gray's discovery, the explorers found the natives racked by disease: malaria, smallpox, syphilis, measles. Their carriers in time infected the Tillamooks as well so that by the 1830s, as noted earlier, only a remnant of the tribe was left.

The Lewis and Clark expedition's first contact with the Tillamooks occurred in January of 1806. Hearing of a beached whale south of

A 1939 photo of Mrs. Ella Center of Garibaldi. The last full blooded Tillamook Indian, she died in 1959, at the age of 97. A granddaughter of Chief Kilchis, the main chief of the Tillamooks, she became a Gold Star mother when her son Frank Mitchell was killed in World War I.

On October 10, 1890, reporting on the passing of a Tillamook Indian named Old Adam, the Tillamook Headlight *wrote the following: "These poor children of the forest are fast passing away, and soon none will be left to tell the tale of persecution and oppression they endured on the advent of our so-called civilization."*

Grace and Joseph Swahaw pose for a formal portrait. Grace was a Tillamook and Clatsop Indian. Joseph was Tillamook.

9

Tillamook Head, Clark, with twelve men and Sacagawea, set out to acquire much-needed blubber and oil. Camping for the night on the head, they began their descent the next morning. It was then that Clark saw the extraordinary vista that he was later to record in his diary and that is the first written description of the site of Cannon Beach: "From this point I beheld the grandest and most pleasing prospect which my eyes ever surveyed."

Proceeding on down the head and crossing the creek, "which I shall call E Co-La or *whale creek*," Clark wrote, the party came upon the 105-foot skeleton of the whale. Returning to the creek and the several cedar plank houses on its bank, Clark found the natives "busily engaged Boiling blubber which they performed in a large square trough by means of hot stones." Clark purchased three hundred pounds of blubber and a few gallons of oil. So laden, the party started out on their return journey to Fort Clatsop. It is the last we hear of the site of Cannon Beach for nearly a century.

ꙅ

But the same cannot be said of the region in which the site lay, for to both the north and south white settlement soon began. In 1810 the fur-trade magnate John Jacob Astor sent out expeditions by land and sea to establish a fur trading post twelve miles in from the mouth of the Columbia, which he named Astoria—the first white settlement in the American West. During the War of 1812, however, Astoria passed to what the Americans called "the plumed bullies of the North," i.e., the Montreal-based North West Company, which promptly renamed the settlement Fort George. Then, with the establishment of the boundary between the Oregon Country and British Canada in 1846, Fort George once again became Astoria. The following year a post office was established, again the first in the West.

The true growth of Astoria did not begin, however, until the first salmon cannery began operation in 1864. By the 1890s there were eleven of these canneries—as well as forty-seven saloons—and a population of nine thousand, making Astoria the third largest city in the state.

Settlement to the south at Tillamook occurred in 1851, when Joseph Champion took up residence in a hollow spruce tree he called his castle. He was followed the next year by Elbridge Trask and several families. By 1853 the place was the seat of a new county, named for the almost extinct tribe, acquiring (some said stealing) all the southern region of Clatsop County up to Arch Cape. But growth was slow; the first public building (a jail) was not erected until 1873.

In time, however, dairying developed, particularly in the form of butter. Lacking Astoria's river to the interior, Tillamook shipped its butter in casks on pack horses over the mountains to the valley, a far from satisfactory operation for a product so perishable. By the last decade of the century, the problem of perishability was solved with the production of cheese. This, together with lumbering and fishing, made Tillamook a prosperous town of 800 by 1890—"a healthy, contented and well-to-do population," according to the 1894 *Oregonian Handbook of the Pacific Northwest*.

Astoria and Tillamook, then, were the principal settlements in the region of the Cannon Beach site. Neither, however, was to have as pronounced an effect on the site as a much smaller place at the south end of Clatsop Plains.

Here, in the early 1860s, on the site of the present Seaside Golf Course, an establishment called the Summer House was opened. It was a resort hotel, possibly the first on the Oregon coast, and operated by a French-Canadian who, it was said, served "French dishes." The Summer House was served by the *Jennie Clark*, a Portland riverboat with a weekly service down the Columbia and into the Skipanon River from which vacationers proceeded by stagecoach to the Hotel.

"Visitors could enjoy the streams and woods, the beach with its cool breezes and the stories told in the evening around roaring fires

11

An 1887 etching of Astoria from West Shore *magazine.*

Astoria, circa. 1885-1888.

Ben Holladay's Sea Side House in 1892, built in 1873 on his 700-acre estate.

A concert for the guests of the Sea Side House. The Sea Side House was torn down in 1922 to make way for the Seaside Golf Course.

13

in the fireplace," according to a memoir by Inez Stafford Hanson. One of the hotel's more frequent guests was a mysterious woman who claimed to be "a countess" and who always carried with her a silver cup in which she insisted all her beverages be served. There is no mention of the nature of the beverages.

In 1873, at the same golf course site, Ben Holladay, the railroad tycoon, built a large luxury resort hotel of fifty rooms called the Sea Side House, which provided as diversions for its guests a racetrack, a menagerie, and, some claimed, ladies of light virtue. At about the same time a post office was established, taking from the hotel the name for the place, Seaside.

Seaside continued to attract vacationers. Many stayed the summer through in little colonies of tents, "the salal and evergreen huckle-berry giving some privacy and easy paths leading to the ocean," wrote the *Oregonian Handbook*. More hotels were built as well, the Grimes House among the most popular.

> Located in a grove on the picturesque banks of the Necanicum and within easy reach of the ocean, nature has done much here toward creating an ideal summer resort . . . the summer home of hundreds of weary city dwellers from Portland and other cities who find here all the comforts of their own homes combined with bracing air and delightful surf bathing.

The *Handbook* also reported on the McGuire House, which advertised "an excellent bar, well supplied with choice cigars and liquors [but] is a separate building from the main house so that it cannot possibly prove of the least annoyance to lady patrons." In general, Seaside had become so favored by vacationers that one commentator called it the "most fashionable summer resort on the Oregon coast."

The popularity of Seaside led to what was perhaps the most important development in the town's history (along with the building of the promenade or "prom" in the 1920s). It was also a development that had a germinal effect on the future Cannon

Beach. In 1890 a railroad of sorts—it operated only in the summer and even then somewhat erratically—was built between Youngs Bay and Seaside. Now saved the jolting stagecoach ride between the Skipanon and Seaside, might not vacationers be tempted to venture a little farther down the coast? Whatever, it could be no coincidence that in the same year as the railroad, a rough road following an Indian trail was driven through the forest from Seaside to what was by then called Elk Creek. And thus with the toll road of 1890 did the present Cannon Beach begin.

CHAPTER TWO

PLACES, LIKE PEOPLE, are often influenced by their beginnings. Early on, both may acquire a certain character that persists through time. Such is the case with Cannon Beach, for at the very beginnings of its history two themes appeared that still today characterize—and divide—the place. These themes were first stated in an article in the *Daily Astorian* in 1891, less than a year after the building of the Seaside-Elk Creek road.

> DOWN TOWARD ELK CREEK: A Promising Section of the
> Country. "There is a pleasure in the pathless woods; there is a rap-

ture on the lonely shore; there is society where none intrudes, by the deep sea, and music in its roar." Probably no finer specimen of what may be considered a sportsman's paradise can be found than that part of the Clatsop coast known as the "Elk creek country," and extending from Tillamook Head to Arch Cape, and comprising Seal rock beach, Brighton beach, and the famous scenery that lies along that famous shore. Is fishing looked for? Elk creek abounds in fish; is hunting the pastime? The hunter can wing an eagle or an elk; a grouse or a bear. All of fur, fin and feather indigenous to this country, is still found there, and the grand old forest, though fast disappearing before the ax of the settler, yet shelter in their shadowy recesses abundance of game. The Elk Creek Road Company have recently put in shape a good road from Seaside, a distance of eight miles from Elk Creek, and those seeking health and recreation can find it in that pleasant locality.

Word comes that a post office has just been established there, a great convenience to the large number of settlers now going into that country, attracted by the fertility of the soil and the beauty of the surroundings. The name of the new post office is Cannon Beach, of which J. P. Austin is postmaster. Well and favorably known from his long residence at Seaside, he is now prepared to receive guests and he and his wife will make comfortable all sojourners in that sunny spot. His team will leave Seaside Tuesdays, Thursdays and Saturdays.

The first theme of the article occurs in the lines quoted from Byron with which the piece begins. Cannon Beach is a place of "*pathless* woods," a place where there is "rapture on the *lonely* shore," a place "where *none intrudes*." In short, Cannon Beach is a place where, to use the old phrase, one can "get away from it all," especially other people.

The remainder of the article illustrates the second theme. It is diametrically opposed to the first, for it is nothing less than a call for tourists! Here is a place for "recreation," for those seeking "a sportsman's paradise" and "the famous scenery that lies along that famous shore." Essential to the enjoyment of all this (both then and now) was what the paper called a "good road" and a place to stay once one got there—in this case the Austin House, which "will make comfortable all sojourners." In short, this portion of the article is simply a promotion, and with the hyperbole common to promotions. In fact, that "good road" was a bone-breaker, while the hotel's "sunny spot" had one of the highest rainfalls in the nation.

So, the two themes. One might be labeled "Come," the other "Stay away." It is an old American dilemma—the desire for Eden, for "wilderness," for solitude in beauty; and the desire for progress, or "development," as we now call it. Nearly a century after the *Daily Astorian* article the *Oregonian* published a similar piece listing the tourist attractions of "The Beach of a Thousand Wonders," as the Chamber of Commerce had dubbed Cannon Beach—a Chamber no doubt much gratified by the *Oregonian's* attention. One citizen, however, who probably reflected the view of others, was not so gratified. "Go away," he wrote to the Portland paper, "and leave us alone. You write stories about us and then everyone will flock down here and ruin things." Of the various themes or threads passing in and out of Cannon Beach history, these are two that have persisted.

The first people who settled in the region of Cannon Beach appear to have shared the rather misanthropic attitude expressed by the letter writer, to have been seekers also after "the lonely shore." The first of these loners was Robert Howell, who settled on Elk Creek in 1850. Twenty years later, homesteaders named Slater and Walters also settled near the creek. By the time the road reached there in 1890, these early homesteads had vanished. Perhaps the region had proven a bit too lonely, too remote, for the only way in or out was the Indian trail that crossed the head to Seaside—not exactly a morning's easy saunter.

However, with the road of 1890 and the official survey of the land done the same year, true and permanent settlement did begin. A dozen families or so, as well as several bachelors, filed homestead claims between present-day Tolovana and Cape Falcon. [1]

Why? According to the *Daily Astorian*, the settlers were "attracted by the fertility of the soil and the beauty of the surroundings." If in fact any had intended to farm in a serious manner, the violent winds and sandy soils would have soon discouraged them. As for the beauty of the surroundings, the homesteaders must indeed have been dazzled by the visual splendor of the place, after all one of the most striking coastal landscapes in the world. Also, they may have been among those who are like iron filings in the sea's magnetic field, that curious, inexplicable attraction that the sea exerts on some, compelling their attendance. Finally, they probably had some inclination toward solitude and the lonely shore, for though the road was an improvement over the Indian trail, their stretch of coast was still a very isolated place.

How did they make out? Information about these early settlers is scanty, but several circumstances may be supposed. They had plenty of timber for their houses, barns, and fences and to burn on stormy nights. In the nearby forests and swamps there were elk, deer, bear, duck, and a plenitude of berries, while in the sea there was a variety of fish as well as mussels, crab, and clams in abundance. Finally, they had their own kitchen gardens, a cow or two, chickens, perhaps a pig. In short, they had the basics: food and shelter.

There were, however, certain things they did not have—a doctor, for example, or a place to buy staples such as flour, sugar, salt, coffee, and kerosene. Thus it was on occasion necessary to travel that "good

[1] These were the Samuel D. Adair family, Robert Astbury, James and Lydia Austin, Rudolph and Emma Bartels, Harry Bell, the Frank Ellis Brallier family, Jacob B. Brallier, the Clark N. Carnahan family, the Sara Clayton family, Anthony Joseph Cloutrie, the John N. Griffin family, Herbert Logan, James Maher, the Leon Mansur family, Rosetta McGuire, Ed McGuire, Robert Norris, Preston S. Philbrick, Osmond Royal, the Bensoh Sabine family, Joseph Walsh, and Edith Watson.

road" to Seaside, an all-day trip. Paul Bartels, son of Rudolph Bartels, who homesteaded at present-day Tolovana in 1889, reported that his father and a friend periodically made this trip. On reaching Seaside, they sometimes found that their exertions had caused a powerful thirst, a thirst they would slake at such establishments as McGuire's, with its "choice cigars and liquors." Arriving back at the end of the day, their funds depleted by the purchase of the staples as well as the "choice liquors," they would avoid the creek's ten-cent ferry fee by wading across "up to their armpits." The staples might get wet but the whisky jug was held high, as was the candy for the children waiting on the creek's far bank.

Among the early bachelor settlers were some who were called "remittance men," defined by the Oxford dictionary as "emigrants who are supported or assisted by remittances from home." The dictionary is too decorous to add that most remittance men were black sheep from the British Isles who were paid by their families to live elsewhere, indeed as far away as possible—even as far away as Cannon Beach.

One of these was an Irishman named James Mehan, locally called Jimmy the Tough. Jimmy was one of the region's first entrepreneurs. His business was to wade out at low tide to the stack called Jockey Cap, fish all day, and then swim back to shore with the evening tide and sell his catch of black cod to the other settlers.

Another of these early entrepreneurs—indeed a true "developer"—was the James Austin mentioned in the *Daily Astorian* article, a long-time postmaster at Seaside who homesteaded a half mile south of Hug Point in 1891. It is said he was drawn to this particular spot because he had hopes of finding the legendary cannon.

In 1846 the U.S. Navy schooner *Shark* foundered in an attempt to cross the Columbia bar. A part of the wreckage to which were attached three cannon drifted south to wash ashore below Hug Point. Several Indians and a U.S. midshipman salvaged one of the cannon and removed it to a creek bed for safekeeping. While they

Above: *"Remittance Man" Joseph Walsh in front of Ecola Creek Hotel.*

Left: *Mark Warren homestead.*

Below: *An early homestead in the Cannon Beach area, complete with wind-blown trees and several tenacious stumps.*

Top: *Jockey Cap, the site of one of James Mehan's (locally known as Jimmy the Tough) entrepreneurial adventures circa 1907.*

Middle: *Mark and Will Warren's original homestead.*

Below: *Will Warrens's first cabin. From left to right: Fanny Thomas, Annie Page, Yick, Mark Warren, Clara Lineberger, Harriet Sayne, Bob Gibson, Will Warren, Emma Sayne, Frank Hamilton.*

were about it, they named the stream Shark Creek and the area Cannon Beach. Whether because of a shifting creek bed or blowing sands or both, the cannon in time was lost to view.

Though Austin's quixotic search for the lost cannon may have figured in his choice of locale, it is probable that a commercial consideration had more to do with it. The place where he and Mrs. Austin erected the region's first hostelry, the Austin House, was about halfway along the Tillamook-Astoria mail route and thus provided an overnight refuge for the intrepid carriers of the mail.

Tourists who made their way to the Austin House must have been intrepid too, for after negotiating the corkscrew turns and deep ruts of the toll road, they were confronted with a hazardous route along the beach. This could only be attempted at low tide, though even then there was no guarantee against a "sneaker wave." Then, too, there was the obstruction of Hug Point. It was a fatiguing climb up and over the point until 1893, when hand and footholds were carved into the sandstone of the cliff. This allowed climbers to "hug the rock"—thus the origin of the point's name.

However, once arrived at the Austin House, visitors apparently found it "comfortable," as the *Daily Astorian* put it. According to the recollections of John Griffin, the hotel was a rustic structure, "homey, quaint, and inviting." Flower baskets hung from the eaves, while a shell path led down between "the gnarled, wind-stunted trees" to the beach. Mrs. Austin, it may be supposed, was a good cook, providing hearty chowders and hot biscuits dolloped with the rich jams made from the woodland berries. Mr. Griffin also remembered that of an evening Mrs. Austin "played on an old-fashioned reed organ" to entertain her guests gathered about the fire. It may well have been worth the hardships of the trip.

But the Austins were not without competition, for another developer was soon to come along—indeed one who had financed and owned the toll road, that first and most germinal development of all. This was Herbert Logan, the proprietor of a sawmill in Seaside. In

1892 Logan left Seaside to build the sixteen-room Logan House (later known as the Elk Creek Hotel) on the north side of the creek at about what is now the corner formed by the Highway 101 Scenic Loop and Fifth Street. Logan was said to be a remittance man and a story told by Bridget Snow suggests that the family that had cast him out were people of some rank. According to Snow, Samuel Adair, who had homesteaded south of Hug Point in 1889, once called at the hotel to find Logan in formal dress seated at a linen-covered table lit by silver candlesticks and attended by a Chinese servant. "He explained [to Adair] that he dined thus occasionally to remind him of home." It was also said of Logan that he was "a heavy drinker." Perhaps he was too far, too long, from home.

Though the Logan House, within hailing distance of the toll gate, was far more accessible than the Austin House, the latter surpassed the former in an important respect. It received that distinction without which a place, in a certain sense, is no place. In 1891 the Austin House, as noted earlier, was designated a post office, for it was there that the mail carriers from Seaside and Tillamook exchanged their sacks—assuming the Seaside carrier had not lost his while hugging the cliffs of Hug Point, as in fact happened on one occasion. As for the naming of the post office, though the cannon sought by Mr. Austin had still not been found, he was determined to commemorate its beaching in his locale and so named his post office for it, Cannon Beach.

It would appear that the first mail route between Tillamook and Astoria was established in 1870. Its southern portion presented many hazards. On those stretches where there was no beach or when stormy weather prohibited its use, the carriers were obliged to travel a narrow trail over Hug and Humbug points, Arch Cape, and False Tillamook (as Cape Falcon was then known) and, finally, make the eight-hundred-foot ascent of Neahkahnie Mountain,

Above: *James and Lydia Austin, the first post masters of Cannon Beach, and owners of the Austin House*

Middle: *The Austin House (and first Cannon Beach Post Office) circa 1891.*

Below: *A 1907 photo of the Elk Creek Hotel, formerly the Logan House.*

where the trail was less than two feet wide in places. In addition, the carriers were often faced with horrendous gales, drenching rains, windfalls, and much mud.

These early mail carriers were the true heroes of the coast. The most remarkable of them, however, was not a hero but a heroine, Mary Gerritse.

Mary was born in New York state in 1872. In 1886, when she was fourteen, her parents homesteaded 160 acres at present-day Manzanita. "I used to split the kindling into tiny pieces and make a flickering light in the hearth of the old box stove to read by. That's when I learned to enjoy Dickens, *Jane Eyre*, Thackeray and Charlotte Brontë." But Mary did more than read. "My father and I milked seventeen cows. At haying time I loaded hay and trod it down and I drove the team, too." Reading, keeping house, milking, haying, and attending a one-room log schoolhouse two miles distant were not her only activities. "We would meet at some cabin and dance all night sometimes." It was at one of these dances that she took a liking to John Gerritse.

John, born in Holland, ran away to sea at fifteen. After sailing around the world "several times," he jumped ship at Astoria, where he soon got a job as mail carrier between Seaside and Tillamook. He must have been a vigorous young man. As Mary said, "It took a week to make the round trip, bringing the mail bag back to Seaside. He would stop sometimes along the way and dance all night. Imagine a man waltzing in rubber boots!"

In November of 1888, Mary, now sixteen, and John, twenty-four, were married. The ceremony was performed on a Saturday, "but we did not have the party till Monday night, as we did not want to have a dance on Saturday night when it would last over into Sunday. We went to church on Sunday. All the neighborhood came to the big party and danced all night till seven in the morning. We had roast beef, chicken pie, potatoes, onions, carrots, milk, coffee, and of course the bridal cake. I had a hope chest but not much to put in it. Mother and I carded wool and filled a comforter with it. John had two good wool blankets. I bought a few sheets in Astoria when I had to make a trip there the week before the wedding to visit a dentist. He pulled two of my teeth. He just yanked them out."

The following year, Mary and John took a claim on the north fork of the Nehalem and built a two-room cabin. "We had a table and a bedstead made of rough lumber with a rope woven across for springs. The mattress was a straw tick. The rough board shelves for clothes I covered with newspapers. I had a few books I brought from home, Dickens, *Pickwick Papers* and *Dombey and Son*. John and I read the Bible clear through one winter." John often went off to Clatsop Plains "to work to replenish the purse in order to buy new housekeeping equipment," and she was alone. "I made my own little world among the big trees, talking to myself and the baby."

Beginning in 1890, the Gerritses made a number of moves—to Stanley Lake between Seaside and Gearhart, Short Sands Beach, and Manzanita, John carrying the mails on and off, homesteading, doing odd jobs. In 1896 Mary spent three months in the hospital "for an operation." She apparently recovered fully, for it was in the following year that she began her fifteen-year career as a mail carrier.

Her husband had once again secured the mail-carrying contract, but due to the work required by his farm he decided to hire a man to take his place on the mail route. "I begged him to let me try it. It would save the man's wages, I was lighter than a man, and I knew how to take care of the horses' backs and saddles." John agreed.

In those first years, Mary had "only a jackknife to defend the mail" and the gallant service of her horse, Prince. From Nehalem to the Austin House, "there were two trails we could follow, depending on the condition of the tide. On both trails we had to leave Nehalem and climb over Neah-kah-nie Mountain on a sheep trail, or an Indian trail, twenty inches wide, down a very steep cut to Cape Falcon. One steep, zigzag trail I always walked to relieve the horse carrying the heavy load of mail sacks. On this hill my white horse, Prince, always stopped and ate several chunks of clay. I don't know why. Perhaps it was salty. The 'Front Trail' strikes the beach on the north side of Cape Falcon. When the tide was low we used this trail over Cape Falcon to the beach, then around or through Arch Cape and along Cannon Beach to Austin's."

Mary experienced many dangers and pleasures on her route. At one point, "the other side of the trail went down four hundred feet to the ocean. I did not know how to be afraid. I lost it all in the woods long before," and so she would stand "watching the wind blowing the enormous waves. Some people are afraid of it, but I loved to stand and let it blow my hair."

On one occasion disaster threatened on the trail. "At a sharp turn where it started along the rim, I always got off and hiked because the trail was so hard for the horse. I got off on the side opposite the canyon. My weight, as I slipped against the side of the hill, threw Prince off his balance, and his hind feet slipped off the trail. The ground was loose dirt on a very steep bank. Prince slipped backward and all his feet went off. He threw himself backwards and lunged to leap back onto the trail, but instead slid down fifty feet, hit a tree, and changed ends. The heavy stock saddle broke his fall so that it did not break his back, but one rib was cracked. When he turned he went around a tree and slid down 150 feet or more to the bottom of the canyon, facing downward toward the ocean three hundred feet below. I knew that if he tried to get up where he landed on a slanting rock, he would slide head first down into the ocean. The mail tied to the saddle probably saved him from being skinned up too badly. I followed right after him and reached there almost as soon as he did. I talked to him to quiet him, but he was so winded at first, he didn't try to move. I broke the brush from around his head, and whenever he started to move I scolded him and he lay quiet. As soon as enough brush was broken that I could turn him around on the rock so that his head was toward the upper part of the canyon. When I talked and pulled on the rope, he would

John Gerritse on his horse.

Mary Gerritse

Mary Gerritse at christening of SS Cannon Beach
with Senator Wayne Morse in 1945.

respond and try to help to get around. Finally he made a big lunge and got to his feet. It had taken two hours to break the brush with my hands and get him to his feet. We followed the creek up the canyon three hundred feet to where I could get him up onto the trail. By that time he was trembling like a leaf. I hiked all the way to Cannon Beach post office and back home twenty-four miles and did not ride him. Prince rested a few days and recovered.

"Prince was a wonderful horse if one understood him. Sometimes I would dally along eating berries and he would get a turn or two ahead of me. If I dallied too long, I would see him coming back peeking around the bushes to where I was. He wouldn't leave and run off like lots of horses."

Despite this near fatality, and others, Mary—and Prince—often enjoyed the trail. "Summer mornings when I went early on account of the tide, I used to get up at 3:30. Then I'd get back to where we had built our cabin on the creek very early in the afternoon. The cabin was gone, but the clover grew deep there. I would stop, loosen the cinch, and take the bit out of Prince's mouth. Then he would have a feast while I lay down and slept for an hour. When he had finished a good lunch and was satisfied, he would come and nuzzle me to say it was time to go home. He never left me and was as near a human being as I ever saw."

In 1904 the Gerritses moved to Seaside, Mary now carrying the mail from there to Cannon Beach. In 1912 she retired. A few years later she and John moved to the present Cannon Beach. There Mary ran a small dairy, though still finding time for good works—helping to found the library, for example. In 1945 she was chosen to christen and launch one of Henry Kaiser's Liberty ships, the SS *Cannon Beach*. No more appropriate choice could have been made. In 1956, at the age of eight-four, Mary Gerritse, one of Oregon's most remarkable women, died. Her full story may be found in the summer and fall 1987 issues of *Cumtux*, the quarterly journal of the Clatsop County Historical Society.

By 1892, the two hotels between Tillamook Head and Arch Cape— the Austin House below Hug Point and the Logan House at Elk Creek— were both accommodating summer visitors. But so far as is known, the first summer visitors to establish an actual residence in the area were a group of related Portland families named Flanders, Glisan, Lewis and Minott. In 1895 they purchased a decommissioned lifesaving station that stood below what is now the parking lot at Ecola State Park. Why had there been a lifesaving station and why had it been decommissioned?

The waters off the Oregon coast, after those at Tierra del Fuego at Cape Horn, are said to be the roughest and most dangerous in the world. The *Coast Pilot* has thrown up its hands and simply written that "the dangers are too numerous for description." Indeed, shipwrecks were so common that the region came to be known as "the graveyard of the Pacific." Thus the necessity for a lifesaving station at Tillamook Head.

In time it became clear that a more effective lifesaving measure would be the construction of a lighthouse. The head itself was first considered as a site, but inspection revealed several problems. For one thing, it was essential for the effective operation of the light that it be close to the level of the sea. But the sea face of the head, in addition to being sheer in many places, was subject to landslides, while the stable benches above were too high and also too often enveloped in fog. Furthermore, servicing the light would have required the construction of a six-mile road through rough terrain, plus the further difficulty of hauling supplies to the road from Youngs Bay, twenty miles distant. For these reasons Major G. L. Gillespie, an army engineer, suggested that the light might better be placed on Tillamook Rock, low to the sea and capable of being supplied by a lighthouse tender.

In 1879 Major Gillespie began his investigation of the rock. He reported: "I finally succeeded in making a close inspection of the rock from the deck of the lighthouse tender, but the ocean swell was so great as to forbid landing. I was enabled, however, to approach sufficiently near to become convinced that the rock is large enough, and the only suitable place for the light."

"On account of other duties" (or perhaps he was intimidated by the size of that "ocean swell"), Major Gillespie delegated further investigation to a Mr. H. S. Wheeler. There was to be no shilly-shallying on the part of Mr. Wheeler. He was instructed, in Major Gillespie's words, "to go to Astoria, and not to return until he had succeeded in landing and taking the measurement of the rock."

Accordingly, Mr. Wheeler embarked on a revenue cutter at Astoria and sailed to the rock. Major Gillespie wrote in his report: "A moderate sea was running in towards the shore at the time, and the waves which broke in the indented surfaces of the rock near the water line made the landing seem a perilous undertaking. The officer in charge of the surf-boat containing Mr. Wheeler and a few sailors daringly approached on the north side, and by running in close on the east side and taking advantage of a small area of comparatively quiet seas, succeeded after considerable trouble and danger in landing two men. They were unable, however, to throw them a line. The seas had begun to run higher and higher; and fearing that the coming storm would separate them from their companions, they jumped into the sea and were rescued by life-lines."

Three days later, Major Gillespie ordered Mr. Wheeler to again attempt a landing (Wheeler had successfully avoided that risk on the first occasion). "The time has come," the impatient major wrote, "when the practicality of landing upon the rock should be determined once for all."

On this occasion Mr. Wheeler did in fact land, clambering up the surf-drenched, slippery rocks; and he did succeed in measuring the rock—measurements that Major Gillespie later denigrated as "imperfect." Nonetheless, they were approximate enough to once again convince Major Gillespie that the rock was a suitable site for

34

Left: *Visiting the Tillamook Rock Lighthouse in an open boat. They are readying the basket to transport someone to the lighthouse.*

Right: *Transferring a visitor from ship to the Tillamook Rock Lighthouse. While the accoutrements may have changed, the method remained the same.*

Below: *A visitor arriving at the Tillamook Rock Lighthouse.*

the light. "Though the execution of the work will be a task of labor and difficulty, accompanied with great expense, yet the benefit which the commerce seeking the mouth of the Columbia River will derive from a light and fog-signal located there will warrant all the labor and expense involved."

And so in the fall of 1879 construction began, and it began with tragedy. John Trewavis, sent to do a construction survey, was swept away by the surf and drowned in his attempt to land. There were problems, too, in recruiting laborers, for employment on the rock meant not only long periods of isolation but hazardous working conditions. "Seas sometimes totally enveloped the rock while men barely managed to cling to their lives," wrote one historian of the rock. As a result, it is alleged, men were bribed, drugged, and even shanghaied to provide a building crew.

Tragedy came to the rock again when on a stormy night, in a flash of lightning, workers saw a three-masted ship heading for the rock. They built bonfires to warn the approaching vessel, but to no avail. The British bark *Lupatia* crashed into the rock and then sank with no survivors but for a collie pup that clambered up the rock to safety. Nineteen days later the light went into operation—nineteen days too late.

The feat of building the light was completed in 1881, and a feat it was indeed. In the face of gale winds and surging seas, twenty-nine feet had been blasted off the top of the rock to provide an eighty-five by forty-five-foot platform for the sixty-nine-foot tower with its 48,000-candlepower lamp, two steam-operated "blasters" (i.e., foghorns), the keeper's house, and the derrick by which men and supplies were carried on and off the rock.

But turbulent times continued for the Tillamook Rock Light-house. Again and again the sea, with its burden of rocks, swept over the top of the tower—134 feet above the sea—breaking the panes of the lantern, piercing the roof, flooding the interior. In view of its tumultuous history, from hot-tempered Major Gillespie down to the lantern's smashed panes, it is little wonder that the Tillamook Rock Lighthouse was the most notorious in the nation and finally came to be known as "Terrible Tilly."

Still, and whatever Terrible Tilly's troubles, the ships at sea were grateful for her light. And as for the people of that village snugged into the lee of Tillamook Head, Tilly's beam sweeping the sea night after night, year after year, became a kind of totem, the beacon of their place.

It was, then, the construction of the Tillamook Rock Lighthouse that led to the decommissioning of the lifesaving station later purchased by the Portland families. Gainor Minott, the only descendant to now live in the area, remembers that in addition to the original structure, there was a wooden chute from the cliff to the beach a hundred feet below, formerly used by the station to lower its lifeboats. In her childhood, horses pulled driftwood up the chute for firewood for the old structure as well as for the two other houses the families had built on the site.

᠆

Three years after the numerous children of the Portland families began to play on the beach at the end of the chute, a momentous event occurred below Hug Point: the long-lost cannon was found. Uncovered by a winter storm, it was spotted by a mail carrier named Bill Luce. John Gerritse brought his team of horses from Nehalem to haul the cannon up and place it in front of the Austin House. Later, it was lodged in the hotel's barn.

Its journey, however, was still not over. At some point it came into the possession of Mel Goodwin, who in 1965 moved it to a site on Highway 101 donated by George Van Vleet, the principal logger of the region. In 1989 it was moved yet again, this time for safekeeping to the Heritage Museum in Astoria—after 143 years returned to the place where its journey had begun. Three replicas of the cannon have been made, two placed at the north and south entrances to

37

The namesake cannon swept overboard from the Shark *in 1846. It was found in 1898 by Bill Luce and hauled to its first home in front of the Austin House by John Gerritse.*

The Hotel Bill, built of logs washed ashore from a broken log raft. It eventually became the Cannon Beach Hotel.

ELK CREEK
·TOLL ROAD·
SINGLE HORSE,
MULE OR ASS__25¢
SINGLE
HORSE & BUGGY_50¢
DOUBLE TEAM__75¢
FOUR HORSE TEAM 1.00$
CATTLE DRIVEN_25¢
SHEEP & HOGS 10¢
H.F.L. LOGAN, Pres.

Above: *A romantic view from the Otto Kraemer property. Otto Kraemer was an historic developer of Cannon Beach.*

Right: *Toll road sign.*

Cannon Beach, the third at the Van Vleet site. The cannon, too, had become a totem.

⟲

A few years after the discovery of the cannon below Hug Point, events occurred to the north of far more importance, at least as a prefigurement of the future. This was more "development." In 1903 Otto Kraemer of Portland and E. Z. Ferguson of Astoria founded the Elk Creek and Cannon Beach Land Company and platted what they called Elk Creek Park, which ran from the creek to Haystack Rock. The fifty by one-hundred-foot oceanfront lots were sold for $100. To encourage development, the partners offered to refund the purchase price to the first person who built a house in the park. Kraemer himself reserved what came to be called Kraemer's Point, just west of the present Coaster Theater, there intending to build his own house. It is said, however, that Mrs. Kraemer objected to the toll road's curves. Well she might; there were 111 of them.

Messrs. Kraemer and Ferguson were not alone in their development efforts. The following year a Mr. Mulhallan filed a claim on Haystack Rock! The size and location of the lots that he envisioned on its precipitous slopes and the design of the houses to be placed on the lots are unknown. In any event, the claim was denied.

There was, too, at the time what was called the Brooklyn Camp. According to Paul Brinkman, it was there, along present Hemlock Street between Van Buren and Monroe, that the first true ensemble of cottages was built. The name of the area allegedly was derived from the fact that the majority of the cottage owners were from the Brooklyn neighborhood in Portland. This might well have been the case, for as late as the beginning of this century, neighbors rather often built their vacation houses in the same locale, thus reproducing their city neighborhoods in whatever coastal or mountain retreat they might have chosen. Now, at the end of the century, with the value placed on "privacy" within our neighborhoods, the sociability

40

and fellowship of our antecedents may come as a surprise. It may come with something else as well, for, having become perhaps too private, having withdrawn too far from community, some may look back with a kind of longing for a place like the Brooklyn Camp.

There were other developments in this first decade of the century as well: Silver Point Cliffs (originally called Sylvan Point), Haystack Rock Park, Arch Cape Park, and Antler Lodge, north of the present Cannon Beach Conference Center. Of more importance at the time was the erection in 1904 of Bill's Hotel on the south side of the creek at the present site of the Conference Center. The hotel was built from logs washed ashore from a log raft that had broken up at sea; the furniture was made from redwood washed ashore as well. Travelers from Astoria left by stagecoach in the early morning to reach Bill's at nightfall. Then, according to one report, "the old stone fireplace was the center of interest, and many fascinating stories were told and yarns spun around its hearth."

In spite of these various developments, as well as Bill's Hotel and the Elk Creek Hotel (the former Logan House), the number of visitors to the area stayed small—to the pleasure of some, no doubt, but certainly not to the region's promoters. The reasons for this lack of growth were simple: the rutted toll road with its 111 curves; there was still no bridge across the creek; and, finally, the rounding of Hug Point remained a risky business.

The first of these problems was attacked and partly solved when some locals urged the improvement of the road as well as its transfer to the county and the dropping of the tolls (which had been twenty-five cents for a horse, ox, mule, or ass; seventy-five cents for a team of horses; and one dollar for a four-horse team). They succeeded. In 1904 the road was "brushed out" and graded, and in 1905 transferred to the county free of tolls. It was an achievement. However, the most significant achievement for the future Cannon Beach had to wait for the end of the decade, when the creek and its environs received what might be called legal recognition.

CHAPTER THREE

In November of 1910, the Elk Creek area was recognized as an official place by no less an authority than the government of the United States. This was signified by the installation of a little cage in one corner of the log-walled lounge at Bill's Hotel, the cage surmounted by a sign that read: "U.S. Post Office, Ecola, Oregon."

Nine years previously the post office at Cannon Beach—which is to say the Austin House below Hug Point—had been closed, which meant that there was no longer a post office between Seaside and Nehalem. This was an entirely unacceptable state of affairs to the

43

residents of the creek, as well as to the region's summer visitors. Accordingly, petition was made to Washington, D.C., for a post office to be established at the creek. The name Ecola was chosen partly to commemorate Lewis and Clark's term for the creek and partly because it was the name unofficially applied to the region by the Portland families on the head.

In the nineteenth and early twentieth centuries, before the time of telephones, the village post office was a valued institution. In addition to the postal services offered, it functioned as a community center where one encountered friends and neighbors (as well as enemies), where gossip and other information was exchanged, and where one might gaze at the faces of notorious criminals who might well be hiding in one's own woods! Also, for some poor widow of the village, the post office could provide work as well as a certain knowledge of other people's affairs and some status, for after all the postmaster was commonly the only representative in the village of the U.S. Government—though at Ecola it was Mr. Lester Bill rather than some poor widow. Finally, the establishment of a post office gave to a place official, legal recognition. For all these reasons the placing of a post office at the creek was considered a major achievement, an important milestone in the development of that little community there in the lee of the Tillamook Head.

∽

In the same year as the opening of the post office, 1910, an organization was formed that can only be described as pro-development. It was called the Push Club. Little is known about the club, but its name tells all. It was formed to push Ecola into the future and all that that might entail. It may be supposed that due to its efforts, at least in part, improvements were made in that aspect of development which has always figured largely in the history of the region. Today it is called "access." In the past it was expressed in a simple, more concrete phrase: good roads. (Indeed, in this period statewide efforts were made to improve Oregon roads, mainly under the auspices of the Oregon chapter of a national organization called the Good Roads Movement. The Oregon chapter's motto was especially pithy: "Get Oregon Out of the Mud.")

The first of these improvements in the vicinity of Ecola occurred in 1910, when a roadway of sorts was blasted out at Hug Point—though it was usable only at low tide. The following year the county began the macadamizing of the Seaside-Ecola road, which, when finished, reduced travel time to thirty minutes! In the same year the creek was finally bridged. Heretofore, crossing had been accomplished by ferry or in the summertime by a rather unreliable "floating bridge." It was in 1912, however, that the most curious road "improvement" of all came about, far-reaching in its effect, and achieved by self-admitted chicanery. Ecola's seashore—for that matter, all of Oregon's seashores—became an official, public highway.

The credit for this unique development goes to one of Oregon's most remarkable governors, Oswald West—a man whose actions, (according to the *Dictionary of Oregon History*) "were sometimes spectacular, sometimes notable but not always without controversy." Indeed.

West grew up in Salem but often traveled about the state with his father, an itinerant cattle dealer. He later became a bank teller, then held several positions in the state bureaucracy. In 1910, he ran for the governorship, announcing that he intended to serve for one term only. An anecdote suggests that by the end of his term he was happy to have so chosen. Calling on his successor, the governor-elect, he informed the latter, who was beaming with anticipation of his term, that once he became governor he would feel as though he had just come down "with a first class case of the clap."

One reason for West's rather jaundiced view of the governorship may have been his failure to entirely rid Oregon of vice, against which he fought mightily. However, he did have a few successes. On one occasion he dispatched his secretary, Fern Hobbs and several

VIEWS OF
ECOLA TOLL ROAD
Right: *A gentleman pre-*
pared for coastal weather
makes his way along the
road in 1907.

Far Right: *Horse-drawn*
cart driven by a woman.

Left: *A 1907 wintry view.*

Opposite page: *A 1907*
traveler with rucksack and
pipe.

Below: *Auto Boulevard*
from Seaside to Cannon
Beach.

High Tide at Hug Point.

A Ford and its passengers destined for Cannon Beach.

Hug Point.

A 1910 campaign photo of soon to be Governor Oswald West.

Oswald West's summer cottage in Cannon Beach.

gun-toting national guardsmen to the town of Copperfield in eastern Oregon with orders to close down all the town's brothels and saloons, of which there were many. And Hobbs, with the help of her armed assistants, did just that (in eighty minutes, she claimed), to the intense irritation of Copperfield's citizens.

Governor West also took action closer to home. The late Harry Teller, a long-time resident of Tolovana, recalled that once in his youth, while he was cavorting in a Seaside dance hall, the governor arrived in his chauffeur-driven touring car, strode into the hall, and announced to the frolicking dancers that he was closing the place down. The dance hall closed down.

Though Governor West conducted no vice raids in Ecola—for, of course, there was no vice in Ecola then or now—he had undoubtedly visited the area while working as a bank teller in Astoria between 1900 and 1903. That he favored the area above all other coastal sites is suggested by the fact that in 1913 he built an impressive log house on the bluffs overlooking Haystack Rock. It may be further supposed that it was the scenic splendor of the area that first convinced him that the beaches of Oregon must be preserved for public use. But how to do so? The Governor laid a trap.

"I knew that any proposed measure to withdraw them [the beaches] from sale [i.e., designating the beaches for public recreation] would attract the attention of upland owners and the legislature would be swamped with protests and the state land board with applications to purchase such lands. So I came up with a bright idea . . . I drafted a simple, short bill declaring the seashore from the Washington line to the California line a public highway. I pointed out that thus we would come into miles and miles of highway without cost to the tax payer. The legislature took the bait—hook, line and sinker. Thus came public ownership of our beaches."

The efforts of the Push Club, together with the road improvements between Seaside and Ecola and at Hug Point, may well have been the impetus that led brothers Mark and William Warren, pioneers of 1893, to build a hotel in 1911 on the present site of the Tolovana Condominiums. William, who had previously served as a steamboat captain in the Alaska trade, named the region of his hotel *Tolovana*, which in an Alaskan Indian dialect means "river of sticks" (though what that name had to do with the area has never been determined.) He also gave Alaskan river names to the streets of his plat.

The Warren Hotel contained sixteen rooms, later supplemented by eight cabins. It was a remarkable establishment in several respects. Paul Bartels—the same who as a child had waited on the creek bank for the Seaside candy—was employed to build the fireplace. Bartels had begun building fireplaces two years previously and was recognized as a master craftsman in the art. For the next half century he built scores of fireplaces, in most of which fires still crackle today. At the Warren Hotel, as for most of his fireplaces, he used what was at hand, the local beach sand and stone. With these he built at the Warren what may have been his masterpiece: a gargantuan fireplace, nine feet from end to end. For many years it would warm the backsides of travelers, as well as the many locals who dropped by the hotel for news and companionship.

The hotel was also distinguished by the whale vertebrae that decorated either end of the veranda and by the Warrens' menagerie of animals: parrots, dogs, cats, a seal and monkeys. There was, however, one minor drawback at the Warren Hotel. If someone drew water on the first floor, no water could be drawn on the second floor—a problem of pressure, perhaps. Whatever, guests apparently were not put off. After all, if the hotel was good enough for its first registered guest, Governor Oswald West, it was good enough, and more, for anyone else.

In addition to their hotel, the Warren brothers figured in another important advance in the area: a water system. Little is known of the enterprise except that it came into operation (though not always to the second story) at the turn of the century and was confined to Tolovana.

In Ecola, on the other hand, a water system had to wait until 1912, when Sylvestor White came upon an artesian spring. White, Captain Orrin Kellog, and Harold McKay then built a system that ran water in wooden pipes from the spring to about Gower Street and mainly served the cottages of the Brooklyn Camp—twelve customers in all, each with a fifty-cent share in the enterprise. Today, piped water is taken for granted. In 1912 the pump could be distant, especially on a day of heavy rains and mauling winds.

A second noteworthy advance occurred in 1915, when a telephone system was installed. Like the water system, it was hardly extensive—only ten party lines. Nonetheless, with water and telephone systems, the citizens of Ecola could now boast that their community, though small and isolated, was getting up to date!

And small Ecola indeed was, fewer than a hundred souls, which probably explains why it had no school until 1912. Then, with the setting up of a logging camp and mill, more children arrived in the community. The first classes were held in Bill's Hotel, then in 1917 were moved to a rented house. Finally, in 1921, a one-room structure was built specifically for the school—though it was sometimes used for church services as well, the separation of church and state being ignored in Ecola.[1]

By now, in the teens and early twenties of the century, Ecola had finally come into its own, no longer a mere wide spot in the road. There were its several hotels filled with summer guests, while on the high ground west of the present main street and also to the south on the bluffs overlooking Haystack Rock, more and more summer

[1] Among the early teachers were Edna Osburn Frisbie, Laura Pratt, Mabel Gillette Longergan, Martha Mosar Barker, Pearl Watson, and Meta Staffan Hunt.

cottages were going up. There were, too, the houses of the full- time residents: hotel proprietors, merchants, loggers, mill workers, a druggist, a mechanic, a carpenter, a teacher. The place could boast telephone and water systems, however modest, as well as a school and part-time church. Ecola was at last a real town.

Unfortunately, there is little record of the daily life of Ecola during this period, but a few events have survived the erasures of time. On October 1, 1913, for example, all who could left Ecola for Neahkahnie Mountain to view the wreck of the *Glenesslin*. A four-master built in Glasgow in 1885, the *Glenesslin* had sailed straight into the base of the mountain in broad daylight during what was called an "Irish hurricane"—a light drizzle on a calm, flat sea. How the *Glenesslin* wrecked under such ideal conditions was a puzzle. Then the explanation came out. The captain, drunk, had handed over control of the vessel to his second mate, inexperienced and thought to have been drunk as well. Both captain and mate lost their licenses for several months and then returned to sea.

The year 1913 witnessed another loss as well. The Elk Creek Hotel, the former Logan House, burned to the ground. Whether Mr. Logan's silver candlesticks were found among the rubble is unknown. However, in the same year Roy Becker, a major landholder in the region, built the Ecola Inn on the site presently occupied by Surfsand. The Ecola (razed in 1966) was known for its ping-pong tournaments and Loleta, the establishment's rather rude parrot.

The following year there was great excitement at another hotel, the Cannon Beach Hotel (the former Bill's, which the Osburns had taken over from Lester Bill). Who should arrive as a guest but Mr. Woodrow Wilson, campaigning for the presidency of the United States! It is unlikely that Wilson considered the Ecola vote crucial to his election. On the other hand, he may well have heard of Ecola's stunning seascapes and in particular of Mrs. Osburn's pie. Her blackberry pie, drenched in the hotel cow's rich cream, had gained considerable fame on the coast.

Primitive but effective advertising for the Elk Creek Hotel, circa 1905.

The proud staff of the Cannon Beach Hotel.

54

Above: *Interior of the Warren Hotel, replete with chairs for all sizes and a Paul Bartels fireplace.*

Right: *Front Porch, Warren Hotel.*

Below: *Hotel exterior with whale vertebra to the left of the porch steps.*

Below: DeWolf & Co. ship Glennesslin, *sails all unfurled on the rocks at the base of Neahkahnie Mountain, October, 1913.*

Above: Seaside's bustling
Holladay Drive at
Broadway circa 1910.

Right: On the beach at Seaside,
circa 1910.

Below: Panorama of Ecola, later
Cannon Beach circa 1910.

Spurred perhaps by the distinction conferred on the Cannon Beach Hotel by the visit of a soon-to-be president, the hotel's principal competitor, the Warren Hotel, took action. The large touring car the Warrens used to convey their guests from and to the train in Seaside was plastered with clam shells and starfish and entered in the Portland Rose Festival Parade. The entry not only won a twenty-five-dollar prize, but also served to remind Portlanders of the Warren Hotel and its locale.

Reaching the Warren Hotel and its stretch of coast continued, however, to entail a wearisome journey of seven and a half hours. This was remedied in 1920, when a paved highway from Portland to Astoria was built along the Columbia River, reducing the Portland-Ecola travel time to only five and a half hours. Further improvements occurred in 1923, when a new and sturdier bridge over the creek was built, complete with a plank sidewalk. In the following year the road itself was extended south of the Warren Hotel. Better and more extensive roads, combined with more ownership of automobiles and the latter's increasing reliability, brought more and more people to the no-longer-lonely shore—to the gratification of some, to the apprehension of others.

෴

During this period an event occurred that was of worldwide significance but which, so far as is known, touched Ecola-Tolovana but lightly: World War I. Surely, however, posters went up in the post office depicting the despicable Hun with blood dripping from his fangs or his bayonet passing through a Belgian baby. Surely, too, shortages of some kind must have been experienced by the locals. It may also be that one or more of the town's boys went off to the battlefields of France. In general, however, the record is silent on the effects of the war on this small, far corner of the nation. The record is far from silent, however, on another event of this period that was of more lasting significance.

It was in 1910, as noted earlier, that the area in the vicinity of Elk Creek was named Ecola. In 1912 the area south of Hug Point called Cannon Beach was renamed Arch Cape. As the years passed—a time before the use of zip codes—the postal service became more and more disgruntled by the number of letters meant for Ecola that ended up in Eola in the Willamette Valley and vice versa. The citizens of the two communities grew disgruntled, too. Accordingly, the residents of Ecola petitioned for a name change in 1922, and since the name Cannon Beach had been abandoned, they took it for their own.

It had taken a long time and many changes. First called No-cost by the Tillamooks, then Ecola by Lewis and Clark, then Elk Creek by the early settlers, once again Ecola by the Portland families on the head and by the postal department, the place finally took for its name the cannon that had washed up not on its beach, but rather at a place called Arch Cape. Such are the confusions of the past. Whatever, the name now was Cannon Beach—and for good, it was hoped.

CHAPTER FOUR

T HE DECADE FOLLOWING WORLD WAR I was a time of prosperity—lots of money made, lots of money spent. It was also a time of social change, especially in the position of women: short skirts, short hair, even the vote. People went to roadhouses and country clubs, danced the charleston and the black bottom, smoked cigarettes and drank Prohibition booze. It was one big party. There were those, of course, who could not afford to attend or were not invited or simply did not care to participate. By and large, however, it was a high old time.

The prosperity, and to some extent the lessening of restraints, was reflected in Cannon Beach in several ways. Prosperity, of course, meant more development. One form of this development came with the increase in motor traffic, and it was called the auto camp.

In the twenties and through the thirties, there appear to have been six or seven of these establishments in and around Cannon Beach, one or more of them owned by Roy Becker. They consisted of "tent houses"—wooden platforms on which tents were erected—or structures that were roofed and floored and walled halfway up with boards, the top half with screening. Each had a stove and sometimes running water. The auto camp office was usually combined with a small grocery, and at some camps there was a dining hall.

The memories of Eve Dye, who worked at one of the camps as a "hired girl," give a sketchy sense of what they were like. The hired girl's first task in the morning was to make the guests' beds and sweep the floors. Next, the lamp chimneys had to be cleaned (no electricity) and the wood boxes filled with kindling. These tasks completed, the hired girl went to the campground garden to gather vegetables and berries for the noon and evening meals, which she later helped to prepare and serve. With the creation of state park campgrounds and the improvement of camping equipment, the auto camps and the hired girl's tasks would pass forever.

During this period there was an increase in another form of development—which, unlike the auto camp, is still with us today. This was the platting of parcels of land into building lots. In the late 1920s, five of these developments were platted in Cannon Beach and Tolovana.

The prosperity, the cheapness of the subdivision lots relative to income, abundant and inexpensive lumber, and the absence of building codes resulted in a great increase in the number of summer cottages in the region. Many were designed in what is called the arts

1912 Cannon Beach tent camp on the Northside of Tanana.

Summer cottages at Cannon Beach.

BEACH HOMES - CANNON BEACH, OREGON.

and crafts style. The highest concentration of these is today on Laurel Street and Ocean Avenue between Van Buren and the town center.

Most of the cottages in this style were wood-framed bungalows with shingled and gabled roofs and overhanging eaves with exposed rafter ends. The exterior walls were shingled as well, left to weather, and inset with small-paned, casement windows. Many of the cottages were fronted with porches or verandas, some enclosed to form sun porches. The chimneys were usually of beach rock, sometimes brick. The interiors were often in the arts and crafts style as well: dark, narrow-paneled wainscoting, plate rails, beach-rock fireplaces, french doors, and wicker furnishings.

The term "summer cottage" is accurate. Most were not constructed for winter use, but rather "opened up" on Memorial Day and "closed down" on Labor Day. The remainder of the year they were left to weather the winter storms. It is remarkable, in view of their construction, that so many have survived the weathering. Today, renovated in the nick of time, they are one of the attractions of Cannon Beach—though their original builders must be rolling in their graves at the prices their two- and three-thousand-dollar cottages now fetch.

The increasing number of summer cottages and the demands of their mainly Astoria and Portland owners, accustomed to the "modern conveniences" of the city, may have been one reason electricity was brought to Cannon Beach in 1925. Its source was a diesel generator installed by the Walter Lyneses in a shed adjacent to their house, which provided current from 6 AM to 11 PM. It is said that Mr. Lynes considerately flicked the lights three times before the current was shut off for the night. The desire for twenty-four-hour service brought Pacific Power and Light to town in 1928. Cannon Beach at last was lit.

There were other material improvements as well. In 1924, as noted earlier, road building had begun south of the town. By 1925 the road had reached Silver Point, the southern boundary of pre-

Above: Eve Dye and her brother Everett.

Right: Eve Dye (she is wearing a watch) with the staff of the auto camp.

sent-day Cannon Beach. Several years later, the road in the downtown was widened to sixty feet. Meanwhile, improvements on the Seaside-Cannon Beach road continued. Roads remained the central factor in the growth of Cannon Beach.

ꙅ

Piped water, telephones, electricity, better and more extensive roads, a variety of commercial establishments (hotels, auto camps, grocers, butcher shops, cafes, a bakery, a drugstore, a filling station, a garage, a lumberyard)—Cannon Beach had by now acquired even more of the material features of a real town. But its facilities were not restricted to the material, for by now the town had its cultural attributes as well. In an organized sense, this began with the formation of the Cannon Beach Civic Club by eight women in 1927.[1]

The club's first project was to provide Cannon Beach with a library. Minnie Nickelsen prevailed upon the state library to send down enough books to stock three shelves in a place called the La Rose Shop. The following year the library moved to a room in a new building built by Mary Gerritse which she rented to the club for $100 a year. The other half of the building's ground floor was occupied by a butcher named Jackson, whose wife, assisted by her two daughters, served as the librarian for the three days a week the library was open.

In addition to the library, the club promoted street lighting, garbage disposal, better roads, and general "beautification." When several of their projects were taken over by the Commercial Club in 1947, the women changed the club's name to the Cannon Beach Library and Women's Club, and as such it continued as one of the town's principal assets. It should be added that there was one project in particular that the club did not hand over to the gentlemen of the

[1.] Louise Bartels, Rose Bingham, Janie Brown, Faye Donaghue, Dora Hardie, Mary Harris, Minnie Nichelsen and Blanche Sheets.

Commercial Club. Every Thanksgiving and Christmas, the women baked a pie for each of Cannon Beach's bachelors.

The appearance of this club in the 1920s and in particular its efforts to establish a library, indicate a change in the character of Cannon Beach. This is not to suggest that all the early settlers, loggers, mill workers, hoteliers, and merchants were lacking in cultivation. One has only to think of Mary Gerritse reading Dickens, Thackeray and the Brontës by a flickering fire in the rough, two-room cabin of her youth. Nonetheless, this demand for a library would seem to mean that by now the town had acquired a degree of refinement that had not been entirely characteristic of its past.

Another instance of this gentling of the community occurred in 1927, when the William Warrens and others gathered to discuss the building of a Presbyterian church. They later purchased property at Washington and Hemlock, and in 1931 the church itself was built by Oliver McClaren. It became, as the years passed, an important institution in the town, its basement often serving as a community meeting place along with the grocery store and post office.

Until the 1920s recreation on the Oregon coast was of a very simple kind: walking on the beach, marshmallow and wienie roasts, and much bathing in the sea. There was, too, crabbing and clamming, both crabs and clams being found in great abundance. Edward Carlson remembers raking in eighteen or so crabs of a morning, while Ted Nickelsen recalls an occasion on which he dug fifty-two dozen clams in the vicinity of Haystack Rock. Then there was berrying in the woods, for salmonberries, blackberries, and huckleberries. Edna Carlson would gather the latter by shaking them from their bushes into an open umbrella. People also strolled the woods for flowers—buttercups, Indian paintbrush, foxglove, the pink buds of the salal—to add to the bouquets of firecracker fuchsia, honeysuckle, and hydrangea from their own gardens. Indoors, people talked by the fire, played games, sang around an upright piano, danced to a gramophone, read, made fudge, did needlework. Then, in the twenties, there appeared in most of the coastal resorts four new diversions, diversions that to some extent would draw people away from the beach and the fireside: the natatorium, the roller rink, the riding stables, and the moving-picture show. Cannon Beach acquired all four.

The Natatorium—the grand Latin name then given to an indoor swimming pool—was built in 1924 by William Mahan. It was located in the area of the present Whale Park and drew its water at high tide from a pipe in the creek.

The Cannon Beach "Nat" had two principal advantages, plus several lesser ones. It was safe (or anyway safer) than the ocean with its undertow and sneaker waves, and it was considerably warmer since Mr. Mahan heated his pool, first with cordwood, later with oil. The Nat also provided four private bathrooms, which could be rented for twenty-five cents—a boon to cottages lacking indoor plumbing and to the auto-camp guests. Bathing suits were rented, too, woolen suits that never seemed to get quite dry. Another attraction of the Nat was the viewing balcony above the pool, for there Mr. Mahan installed a nickelodeon—a primitive form of jukebox—and thus the balcony became a place to dance.

Summer after summer for the next twenty years, the Nat would be a place of delight, echoing with the whoops and cries of the bathers, the blaring jazz tunes, the stomp of the dancers' feet. When World War II shortages of chlorine and heating oil forced the Nat to close, something more than the old pool and its raftered ceiling passed, something that reflected an interesting difference between then and now. People did not go to the Nat to exercise, to "get in shape" by swimming so many laps, and they certainly did not go to train for some competition. They simply went to play together in the water.

The Nat's principal competition during its heyday was the roller-

Cannon Beach's swimming pool (natatorium), on the right, with its heated seawater.

Yet, the unheated surf still held its appeal.

skating rink, built by Ray Walker on the site of the present Coaster Theater. The two institutions had certain things in common. Both were places where girls could meet boys and boys could meet girls. Perhaps more important, both were places where boys could show off in front of girls—a jackknife high dive or a graceful swoop at breakneck speed on one skate. Both places, too, provided music, at the rink a steam calliope that played melodies suitable for the execution of the figure eight marked out on the rink's maple floors. Finally, both Nat and rink were the sites of the first moving-picture shows in Cannon Beach. Mary Shields remembered that at the Nat they were projected on one of the outside walls, the audience bringing their own seats in the form of apple boxes.

The fourth popular diversion to appear in the 1920s was the riding stables, one on the banks of the creek, another south of Ecola Inn. To stock their stables, the Spaulding family drove their horses all the way from Yakima, a two-week ride, camping along the way. Closer at hand was the Osburn family from Astoria, whose stables were known in particular for their "dinner rides." For one dollar, customers were offered a leisurely trot along the beach, preferably at sunset, followed by a bonfire and barbecue. There were also people who brought down their own horses by riverboat from Portland to Astoria, riding on from there to Cannon Beach.

It could add up to a very full day: a swim in the morning, a skate in the afternoon, a ride in the evening, a moving-picture show at nightfall, all topped off by a little dancing at the Nat.

Looking back, some view the twenties as a golden age for Cannon Beach. For one thing, there was growth. "The advancement of Cannon Beach," wrote the *Astoria Evening Budget*, "has been the most striking . . . in Clatsop County." The locals made money while the summer people found all manner of recreation, many remaining in their cottages all through the summer. "The head of the household," as he was often then called, would join the family for the weekend, arriving at Seaside on one of the "daddy" trains from

At the Seaside Railroad Station with the Seashore Limited or "daddy" train.

The Ecola Inn with visiting riders.

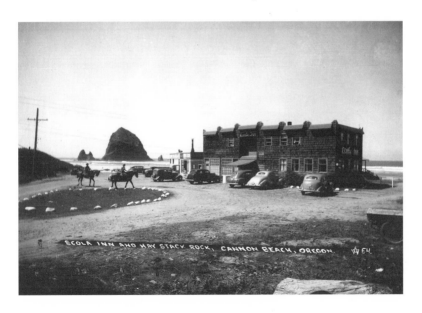

Portland and Astoria. The remainder of the week the family was on its own.

Marion Pattullo remembered it as a carefree time. "I often think of what a snap my mother and her sisters had. We would go down [to the beach] in the morning and take a lunch with us and we would build a sandcastle all day long. They could look out the window and see where we were . . . so they had a lovely day to do what they liked to do and we had a lovely day to do what we liked to do."

As the afterglow of evening softens the landscape and brings tranquility, so too the afterglow of the past may reflect a time of untroubled serenity—and thus obscure the harshness, grief, and discord that are part of any time. A child lost to the outer surf, a love affair gone wrong, a beloved cottage burning to the ground, the arrival of a weekend husband dreaded. Still, there are good times and bad times, and those years at Cannon Beach seem in general to have been the former—especially when compared with what was to follow.

Although events in Europe in the late teens (World War I) had little apparent effect on Cannon Beach, events in New York at the end of the twenties—the stock-market crash of 1929 and the Great Depression that followed—had a much greater impact. The locals, whether hotelier or carpenter, grocer or developer, lost much of their income. "Most people were out of work," Tom Turner recalled. "The diet of most people was clams, crabs, and even mussels." Harold McKay remembers that the goal was simply "to survive." The summer-cottage owners were hard hit as well. Some were forced to sell at a loss, while other cottages were repossessed by the banks. And in 1931 Clatsop County urged Cannon Beach to incorporate so that the strapped county would be saved the cost of street repair. The town grew shabby, and on those lowering afternoons of winter it looked and was a depressing place indeed.

But now and then the sun—metaphorically speaking—broke through. One of these breaks took the form of an ancient remedy for depression: with the end of Prohibition in 1933, what had been the Imperial Grill became Bill's Tavern.[1] Ted Nickelsen recalls that a small beer was a nickel, a large beer a dime—assuming you had the nickel, let alone the dime.

However much the beverages purveyed by Bill's Tavern may have lifted the gloom, at least for some, a far more enduring break in the clouds occurred in 1932 due to the generosity and acumen of six people. One of them, like Governor Os West, belongs in the Oregon pantheon: Sam Boardman.

Boardman, of the town of Boardman, Oregon, was appointed the state's first superintendent of parks in 1929. By the time his tenure ended in 1950, he had been the force behind the creation of 181 state parks. Of those, his greatest achievement was Ecola State Park.

The achievement could not, however, have taken place without the generosity of the descendants of three of the Portland families who had established summer houses on the head in 1895: Rodney Glisan, Florence Minott, and Carolyn and Louise Flanders. "We have had many gifts of a recreational nature," Boardman wrote, "but never one that so involved pure sacrifice of such a beautiful setting and lovely houses."

As for the descendant of the fourth family, Allen Lewis, he was not, Boardman wrote, "in a giving mood." Thus the state was obliged to come up with $17,500 for Lewis's 51 percent share of the 450-acre parcel. However paltry $17,500 may seem today, it was by no means paltry in 1932, in the depths of the Depression when, as Governor Julius Meier put it, the state was "dead broke." Acceptance by the Parks Commission was no sure thing.

[1] The distinguished authority on Oregon coastal ghosts, Abel Heart Kloster, states that Bill's Tavern—and possibly the Coaster Theater—is the only haunted structure in Cannon Beach. The tavern, once much patronized by loggers, is haunted, according to Kloster, by the ghost of a logger who on occasion peers in the window with disdain at the tavern's present clientele.

Right: Samuel Boardman, Oregon's first superintendant of parks. Ecola State Park was created during his tenure.

Below: The former lifesaving station at Ecola State Park.

Rodney L. Glisan and Mrs Rodney Glisan, (nee Elizabeth R. Couch),
Miss Caroline C. Glisan at Ecola Point, July 1914.

This was the view the Glisans, Minotts, and Flanders gave to the state of Oregon in
1932. Samuel Boardman wrote, "We have had many gifts of a recreational nature,
but never one that so involved pure sacrifice of such a beautiful setting.

"There were some 300 people in attendance at this Commission meeting," Boardman wrote. "Before I could explain why Ecola Park should be accepted, one of the Commission jumped to his feet and proceeded to give me one of the most complete verbal tongue lashings my august person has ever been decorated with. Times were tough at this time and the Commissioner thought it sacrilegious to be spending money for parks when people were tottering on the verge of starvation. His face was as red as mine was white. In some manner, I feathered my wings until the gust passed by. The Commission then voted to accept the park. While the drama was at its height, a bit of humor crept in. Chairman Ainsworth was softly trying to lessen the temperature of the speaker, when Commissioner 'Sage' Hanley (*Feeling fine*) [due to imbibing an unknown beverage] without looking right or left said 'Let the monkey climb the pole, he'll slide back down.' All three members of this Commission are on the board of directors of the Lord's Golden Streets. May the living ever pay homage for their foresight in obtaining this ocean wonderland." At the close of his career Boardman wrote, "Never let the marrow of your backbone solidify. Never let your vision be grounded." He did not.

"In the belly of evil there is good," goes an Arab proverb. One of the good things to come out of the belly of the Great Depression was the Civilian Conservation Corps: paid employment for out-of-work young men, living army style and engaged in public works. Beginning in 1934 the CCCs, as they were known, worked on the dedicated land to create a park—a new approach road, parking lots, a water system, trails, viewpoints, picnic tables, restrooms, and shelters. By 1935 the park was finished.

It is said that on dedication day in Cannon Beach, twenty-five hundred well-wishers were served coffee and clam chowder while five hundred couples danced to a brass band on festooned Hemlock Street. Cannon Beach went wild and indeed it was an event to go wild about—to have at the entrance to one's town one of the most scenically stunning parks in the world. Rodney Glisan, Florence

76

Minott, Carolyn and Louise Flanders, Sam Boardman, and the men of the Civilian Conservation Corps are to be remembered.

༄

There was yet another enduring break in the clouds during the Depression period. In 1936 a contract was signed for a tunnel through Arch Cape. On its completion, Cannon Beach would no longer be "the end of the road" but rather a place people would pass through but where, it was hoped, they would pause and spend some money, perhaps even stay a night or two. Most people considered the tunnel a boon but there were others, of course, who feared that Cannon Beach would be "discovered." Why, there were already over a hundred full-time residents! Progress? As usual, opinion was divided.

༄

Good times, bad times. Nature itself played an accompaniment to each. In 1927 and again in 1933, there were several serious landslides. Such slides were chronic to the Cannon Beach hillsides and cliffs, the soft mudstone of the bedrock, cut-and-fill terracing, septic-tank drainage, and the heavy rains all contributing to their frequency. Even more frequent, almost yearly, was the flooding of the downtown caused by storm tides flowing up Elk Creek, spilling into what was then the low swampland east of the main street, and finally receding into the main street itself. However, the most damaging of nature's bad times occurred in the first week of 1939, when fierce winds, drenching rains, and a raging surf tore away the seafront gardens of several Cannon Beach cottages.

But nature had its good moods, too, like Cannon Beach itself, days when the sea was blue as lapis, the surf a distant sigh, the sun streaming down to turn stone and sand, shake and shingle, everything, pale gold, even the wind dropping to no more than a gentle zephyr— perfection. Good days and bad.

CHAPTER FIVE

IN THE 1930S AND EARLY 1940S, several events occurred that would end the isolation of the Oregon coast—a relative isolation, of course, not absolute. After all, the first place in Oregon occupied by whites had been the coast, in the time of Lewis and Clark and the Astorians. Then there were the gold strikes of the 1850s on the southern end of the coast and, in the 1860s the gold of canned salmon on the northern coast, both developments bringing the outside in.

Nonetheless, the coast remained sequestered relative to the interior. In part this was due to geography: the coastal mountains, few good harbors, and some of the roughest waters in the world. Economic factors played a part as well. There was little good agricultural land and, compared with many coasts, little fishing except for salmon. (Oregonians have never been great fish eaters, unlike many maritime people—the Japanese, for example.) For all these reasons, the coast remained sparsely populated and little visited.

With the advent of paddle wheelers on the rivers, railroads from the interior, and roads of a sort over the mountains, the coast slowly began to open to the outside and in particular, as we have seen, to vacationers. But it was not until 1933 that the trickle became the beginnings of a flood, for it was then that Highway 101 was completed along the coast. Motorists were no longer obliged to take to the beach, or wait for ferries at the coast's major rivers after these were crossed in 1936 by C. B. McCullough's six beautiful bridges.

Then, in 1940, the tunnel through Arch Cape was completed. This was of the greatest importance to Cannon Beach, for it put the town on Highway 101, this coastal road that now extended from Canada to Mexico. Previously, 101 had skirted Cannon Beach at the Cannon Beach Junction, passing inland to the Necanicum Junction and thence along what is now Highway 53 to Nehalem. Now, with 101 rerouted to pass through Cannon Beach, the town was no longer a dead end but "on the way"—a circumstance that in 1941 led Oregon Motor Stages to provide a through service south. The new service, with a bus grandly christened "The City of Cannon Beach," was inaugurated by Miss Crystal Jackson in a blue satin swimsuit provided by the Library and Women's Club. Photos of Miss Jackson in her swimsuit were widely distributed—the bathing beauty, that figure which has beckoned men to the coasts of the world for as long as women have gone into the sea.

In 1941 another significant highway improvement occurred with the construction of the Wolf Creek Highway from about Manning to 101 at the Necanicum Junction. This reduced travel time from

Left: Crystal Jackson on christening day for the City of Cannon Beach bus. Her father had a butcher shop in the Gerritse building which now houses the White Bird Gallery.

Below: Crystal Jackson and her unnamed companions look on as a bottle swings toward a sturdy Firestone tire to christen the bus.

Portland to Cannon Beach from five and a half hours on Highway 30 along the Columbia to two and a half hours on the Wolf Creek. It also reduced, though it did not eliminate, carsickness, for although Highway 30's curves could be avoided, the 111 curves from the Cannon Beach Junction to Cannon Beach remained.

The major highway improvements, more reliable automobiles, the innovation of the paid vacation, and the "thirty-nine things to do from Ecola Park to the Penny Arcade" touted by the Cannon Beach Directory (not to mention the opening in 1941 of a saltwater-taffy shop, which no respectable seaside resort could be without)—all these ended for good "the lonely shore." The future, especially the tourist future, looked very bright indeed.

The weather at the Oregon coast is noted for its changeability; thus the coastal saying that if you don't like the weather, wait ten minutes. This changeability sometimes extends to human affairs as well. In less than a year, the brightness of that tourist future was obscured by a cloud, a cloud that would not lift for another four years. On the afternoon of December 7, 1941, those in Cannon Beach who were listening to their radios heard through the static the appalling news. The Japanese had bombed Pearl Harbor. World War II had begun.

As noted earlier, World War I did not, so far as is known, have a significant impact on Cannon Beach. Among other things, it was far, far away, on the other side of the Atlantic. But this war raged in the Pacific, that ocean which thundered only a few yards from Cannon Beach's main street. The enemy might appear on the horizon at any minute!

As Les Ordway and George Shields remember, the locals immediately took action, forming a beach patrol called "the Guerrillas" as well as placing guards at the Arch Cape tunnel. Also a blackout was enforced and headlights wired down. Other communities on the

Hemlock Street circa 1940. A view looking south. The building with the second-
story porch housed Jackson's Meat
Market and the library.

Looking north circa 1940. Boardwalks are still in evidence as the citizens pass by
Don Newman's Drug Store, the Cannon Beach Bakery and the post office.
Further down the road is Bill's Tavern.

Cannon Beach flooded often before the dike was built.

83

coast took similar precautions. World War I veterans at Tillamook organized the Tillamook Rangers. Equipped with shotguns and .22s, the Rangers drilled on the beach, ready for the enemy.

As might be expected under the circumstances, the first months of the war saw occasional bouts of hysteria. For example, some people fled to the interior on hearing the rumor that five thousand Japanese paratroopers squatted atop Marys Peak waiting for Emperor Hirohito's order to descend on the coast. In Cannon Beach a number of families provided themselves with "grub boxes," provisions packed and ready for flight to the hills. Then there was the shelling of Fort Stevens by a Japanese submarine in June of 1942. Though not understood at the time by the population at large, this was no more than an act of bravado, a tweaking of Uncle Sam's whiskers, for the Japanese well knew that their deck gun could do little damage. Still, the audacity of the attack reinforced local fears. More serious were the tiny Japanese collapsible-wing airplanes carried by some submarines, which dropped incendiary bombs on coastal forests.

In view of these Japanese thrusts, it was perhaps as well for the lone Japanese family living in Cannon Beach that they were removed shortly after Pearl Harbor. It was said that the man, who operated a knick-knack shop, was much given to photographing the coast. Whether his motives were aesthetic or he was engaging in espionage was never determined, but, as might be expected under the circumstances, the latter explanation was the one more favored. Thus the relocation of the Japanese throughout the West touched Cannon Beach.

Following the Battle of Midway in June of 1942, fear of a Japanese invasion abated considerably. In the meantime, regular forces had been garrisoned along the coast. First the Army and then the Coast Guard took over the Cannon Beach Hotel and the Warren Hotel, and for the duration of the war the latter patrolled the beach on foot and horseback. They were supplemented by aircraft spotters, Cannon Beach women who were installed in huts along the beach and provided with silhouettes of enemy aircraft.

All these circumstances, together with the departure of local young men and women for the service, brought the war home to Cannon Beach.[1] In addition, the rationing of gas and tires greatly depleted the number of Portland tourists. There was, however, a partial compensation: the personnel stationed at Astoria's naval base, air station, and hospital, as well as the troops at Fort Columbia, Fort Stevens, Fort Canby, and Camp Rilea, found "The Beach of a Thousand Wonders," as Cannon Beach now styled itself, an appealing change from barracks life. And there were plenty of accommodations—232 locations with rental cottages according to the 1941-42 Cannon Beach Directory. The names of many of these cottages illustrate the degree to which the sea air can stimulate the imagination. For example: Bonnie Nook, Bide-A-Wee, Burrow Inn, Cuddle Doon, Glory-Be, Grain-O-San, Huddle Inn, In-Fer-Fun, and Oh-Kum-Inn.

With the ending of the war in 1945, Cannon Beach, like the rest of the nation, turned its attention to some long-delayed improvements. In the case of Cannon Beach, the first of these was sidewalks. Because of the downtown's problem with flooding when heavy rains and high tides combined to overflow the banks of Elk Creek, its wooden sidewalks had been built some two feet above ground level. (It is said that boys were wont to lurk beneath these raised walks in order to spy on passing ladies through the cracks in the boards—though some, like George Shields, insist that they were only looking for any loose change a passerby might have accidentally dropped.) Now the town's boardwalks were replaced with asphalted berms. Boardwalks were an old-time feature of Oregon's coastal resorts. The new sidewalks signified as much as anything the passing of an era.

[1] Many of the names of those from Cannon Beach who served in the war may be found in the George Shields interview on file at the Cannon Beach Historical Society.

Another important event of this immediate postwar period was the founding of the Cannon Beach Conference Center, one of the town's more interesting institutions—and one of its oldest, for in 1995 the center celebrated its fiftieth anniversary. It began when Archibald McNeil, a Portland minister, and his wife, Evangeline, purchased the Cannon Beach Hotel from the George and Edna Frisbie family in 1944. Their purpose was to create a church camp that would be interdenominational, unlike Oregon's many other church camps. Also unlike many church camps, much leisure was provided along with the religious programs. According to Heather Goodenough, the McNeils' daughter, who ran the center for some years, her father believed that "the mind can only absorb what the seat can bear." In general, the center proved a great success. Beginning with the fourteen hotel rooms and four one-room cottages, the center through the years added a number of volunteer-built structures, which now provide over one hundred rooms for the participants in its varied religious programs. In a quiet way, the Cannon Beach Conference Center is an important and distinctive strand in the many strands that make up Cannon Beach life.

Shortly after the opening of the Conference Center, there were two other important developments. The first had its impetus in 1946 when a house in town burned to the ground (not the first, by any means) and an occupant died either in the blaze or, by another account, later of shock. This calamity, together with the recognized ineffectiveness of buckets and garden hoses, finally brought home to the town the need for a fire department.

This may have been one of the factors that in the following year led Kenneth Cole, Louise Durkin, Les Ordway, and Duncan Shields to found the Commercial Club. Since Cannon Beach was unincorporated and thus had no governing or taxing body, it was in need of an organization to promote and provide for the town's basic services. Such was the Commercial Club's goal, though in addition it hoped to encourage various social activities.

The Clatsop County bookmobile circulated through Cannon Beach
during the 40s. The boys waiting in line for books are Cheg Vilever, Alan Becker,
George Shields, and Thurman Campbell.

This photo ran in the Oregon Journal *October 7, 1942 with the following caption*
"These girls are using the famous cannon which give Cannon Beach its name to
put over what seems to be a new version of walking the plank."

One of the club's first tasks, prompted by the tragic fire, was to provide for a fire department. In this it was greatly assisted by James Hicks, a Portland fire captain who had retired in Cannon Beach. Captain Hicks prevailed on an eastern Oregon town to donate an outmoded engine, Si Hoffman was chosen as fire chief, and seventeen volunteers were signed up, including Les Ordway, Bob Rittenback, and Bud Stevens. Finally, this community of wooden structures fanned by the ocean breezes was provided with that most essential of services, a fire department.

The Commercial Club also helped establish other important services. For example, it collected money to keep the street lights functioning, a service that had foundered despite the attempts of the Women's Club to maintain it. Then, because of the infrequent presence of lifeguards and the occasional drowning of swimmers, the club, in conjunction with the new fire department and the Coast Guard, organized a beach patrol under the direction of Delno McCoy. McCoy's service was so outstanding that following his death in 1968, a truly dramatic tribute to him was organized by the beach patrol and the Coast Guard. A plaque commemorating his service was dropped into the sea by a Coast Guard helicopter. The beach patrol then swam out to the flagged plaque, retrieved it, brought it back to the beach, and presented it to McCoy's widow. It cannot be said that Cannon Beach is without flair.

Like many communities across the nation, Cannon Beach arose like a phoenix from the fires of war and with new and important institutions, such as the Conference Center and the Commercial Club, and important improvements such as sidewalks, street lighting, a fire department, and a beach patrol. Also, of great importance to the increasing accessibility of Cannon Beach was the construction in 1948 of a new highway linking Portland with the Wolf Creek Highway at Manning, both stretches now called the Sunset Highway.

In the same year, local improvements included the expansion of Ecola Park to encompass one thousand acres and the installation of dial telephones. It was in 1949 and 1950, however, that the phoenix really flew.

Fortunately, there is a record of that flight in a Cannon Beach newspaper of the time called the *Cannon*.[1] Jim Dennon, a seventeen-year-old high school student, started the *Cannon* in the back room of his parents' grocery on a hectograph, a device for making copies from a gelatin plate. The paper was first intended for the grade school students and sold for three cents a copy.

Due to what might be called its rather quirky quality, the paper caught the attention of adults, and the attention increased when Dennon began to devote much space to the highly controversial subject of incorporation. Graduating from the hectograph to a mimeograph to an actual printing press, Dennon's *Cannon* finally became a full-fledged small-town paper.

In addition to covering the local news, the *Cannon* conducted surveys. For example, a poll taken at the grade school found that the majority of male respondents desired "more girls and more sleep." The *Cannon* also took firm editorial positions. With regard to an approaching school levy, the paper was very firm indeed. "Why do we at Cannon Beach always have to be the victims of a *PARSIMONIOUS* minority." "You are your brother's keeper," the editor continued. "We have no place for a Frankenstein."

The paper also welcomed letters from readers. When these were lacking, it may be that they were supplied by the editor himself under a nom de plume. For example: "If you want a wholesome treat and a healthy treatment, go to the Roller Skating Rink and meet the gracious Mr. and Mrs. Walker, the apparent owners . . . and

---

[1.] Cannon Beach has had several newspapers of varying quality and tenacity. The first, *The Ecola Echo*, was produced by the CCCs. There was as well *The Cannon Report*, *The Cannon Ball*, *The Pacific Arch*, *The North Coast Times Eagle*, and a magazine called *Whalesong*. The present publications are *The Cannon Beach Gazette* and *The Upper Left Edge*.

watch the genial, patronizing and instructive Schade boys skate their attentive and instructive stuff. It is a pleasure to spend a couple of hours there by reason of the fine manners observed and the created atmosphere of propriety that pervades the place. It provides a fine evening of entertainment for the spectator as well as the skaters. Seats are provided and upon leaving a friendly 'Good night' is accorded to you with an invitation to 'Come again.'" Signed: Adame Goode Reeder.

The *Cannon's* principal purpose, however, was to report the news—and there was much to report, especially in 1949. The bowling alley and penny arcade, owned by N. D. Jacobson—also owner of the local lumberyard—received "a nice coat of white paint." The grade school received a new gym, the American Legion a new hall, the women of the town a new beauty parlor, and the fire department a new resuscitator. "As 1949 went over the hill," wrote Dennon in January of 1950, "Cannon Beach is left a changed 'city,' indeed with a growth unequaled perhaps of previous years; new business, new buildings, increased population (about 500), new streets, new utility improvements, a new highway, a new outlook for 1950."

Perhaps the most important of these developments listed by Dennon was the "new highway," for this referred to the elimination of a drawback that had plagued Cannon Beach from the beginning: those 111 nausea-causing curves between the junction and the town. Completed in 1950, the new road (which reduced travel time from Portland to an hour and a half) had several interesting effects. For one thing, up until the 1950s, retirees had tended to shun Cannon Beach because it lacked medical facilities. Now, with travel time to Seaside and Astoria much reduced, that was less the case.

The new accessibility also stimulated the promoters of tourism to activity. Already in 1949, in anticipation of the new road, advertisements for "The Beach of a Thousand Wonders" were broadcast on a Portland radio station. And in the following year this notice appeared in the *Cannon*: "Business people and citizens of Cannon

Beach: A meeting will be held Thursday evening, Jan 19 at 8: P.M. *sharp* in the Community Hall for the purpose of advertising Cannon Beach and promoting off season trade. Everybody welcome."

"Everybody" was perhaps an exaggeration, for there were some who probably would not have been in the least welcome—for the reason that the old debate had surfaced again. The *Cannon* quoted one person, identified only as a "poet," as saying: "I sincerely hope that Cannon Beach will at no time in the future become as contemptible and commercial as certain coast resorts nearby."

Then there was the case of the late John Yeon, a distinguished Oregon designer and a major owner of oceanfront property in Cannon Beach. In an interview, Yeon recalled that at that time he was considered "a city menace because I was anxious to preserve undeveloped land. And all the boosters and movers of Cannon Beach were all for greater development, attracting more people. And they said, 'Wilderness, we got too much wilderness around us. Why do we want to preserve any more.'" Yeon also recalled that at one hearing someone had said, "One man shouldn't own all that land," while another complained that Yeon's "no trespassing signs give Cannon Beach a very inhospitable air."

As it turned out, both sides in this chronic Cannon Beach controversy suffered a victory and a defeat. The boosters had finally gotten rid of the 111 curves that for so long had inconvenienced tourists; but it was, of course, an improvement deplored by those who thought that the fewer tourists the better. On the other hand, the boosters were dismayed to find that the new road, on reaching the approach to Cannon Beach, turned aside from the town to run along the high ground to the east, relegating Cannon Beach proper to a "scenic loop" *off* Highway 101. This, of course, was a consolation to those who favored Cannon Beach's seclusion. The latter were also heartened that now, in 1950, driving on the beach was for the first time subject to at least some control. On one point both sides agreed and were relieved. The log trucks no longer rattled

91

Above: *In the summer of 1951 Bob McKinney (left) and Baylor Lowe proudly serve as Cannon Beach Lifeguards.*

Opposite page *This 1950s California fantasy vanished as controls for cars on the beach tightened.*

Below: *This 1966 beach rescue is a credit to Delno McCoy who organized the beach patrol.*

An aerial view of Cannon Beach's post war growth.

93

every window in the town when they passed through—and they had passed through often.

᠀

In the fall of 1950 Jim Dennon, now graduated from high school, joined the army, and with his departure the *Cannon* ceased publication. But Dennon's interest in his town did not cease. Indeed, upon his return from the service, that interest greatly increased, taking the form of his chronological history of Cannon Beach and his work as a founder of the Cannon Beach Historical Society. Without the late Jim Dennon's research, this book could not have been written.

᠀

The fact that Dennon's *Cannon* gained popularity among adults when it began to deal with the question of incorporation shows just how thorny that question was. First proposed in 1931 by Clatsop County and rejected, incorporation again became an issue in 1948, when the town's sewage became a problem. On occasion it flowed onto the beach.

Despite this odoriferous overflow, there was much opposition to incorporation, and it was voted down four times. Opponents argued that the town did not contain sufficient assessed valuation to support municipal government. Feelings ran high. In January of 1950 an anonymous handbill appeared in the town: "Don't Be Misled: Incorporation Means Added Expenses and *Higher Taxes*. The benefits would accrue to a few who would promote their personal interests at the expense of the other residents." More serious evidence of strong feelings appeared in the *Cannon*: "If we have amongst us anyone who would boycott a local businessman because of his political views, he should hang his head in shame."

Meanwhile, the sewage continued to overflow. At one point the state health authorities threatened to post the beach as contaminated. This, plus the fact that federal funds to help correct the problem could be obtained only if Cannon Beach were to incorporate, finally got the measure passed in 1955—with a plurality of only four votes out of the total of 303 cast. Thus did the village of Cannon Beach become the City of Cannon Beach, a term that pleased some, saddened others.

The first major effect of incorporation—aside from sewer construction—was the employment the following year of a policeman. He was given a salary of sixty-five dollars a month and was expected to provide his own car. However, it took two years before a city charter could be agreed upon. A Tillamook judge who attended the charter meetings said he had never encountered such profound and prolonged disagreement, which no doubt explains the hiatus between incorporation and enactment of a charter. The charter called for a strong chief executive, i.e., a mayor with considerable power. In view of the past controversies it may have been felt that a firm hand was needed.

ᔕ

Though the enactment of a city charter in 1957 was a significant addition to the history of Cannon Beach, there was also in that year a significant subtraction. Terrible Tilly's light was extinguished, her fog horns silenced, both replaced by an automated buoy at sea. For seventy-six years Tilly's light had swept the sea, her horns moaning through the fog-bound night. For those who had lived their lives in Cannon Beach, for the summer people too, the horns and the light were as much a part of the place as the head itself. For these now to cease, never to shine and sound again, was a wrenching thing. To some it was a sign.

ᔕ

In certain places weather has a force, a prominence, almost a personality, that it lacks in others. This is the case on the Oregon coast. It is due in part to the extreme changeability of the weather, but even more so to the violence that the coastal weather often exhibits.

As noted earlier, slides and flooding in Cannon Beach had been chronic from its beginning, and the storm of 1939 did severe damage to the sea front. The 1940s saw dangerously high tides and punishing storms as well, and in 1949 forest fires, spread by ocean winds, nearly engulfed the town. In 1951 Cannon Beach braced itself against an eighty-mile-an-hour wind, and in 1953 it again suffered an unusually violent storm. Then, in March of 1961, with the highest rainfall on record, a devastating slide occurred at Ecola Park, a large section of the picnic area plunging into the sea. But none of these occurrences equaled in drama and destructiveness the events of Easter week 1964.

It was just before midnight. Marie Marshall, in her bath, wondered why on earth the lights went out. Margaret Sroufe, glancing out her window, saw what looked like a meteor blitz of blue and green orbs. Bridget Snow and her husband hurried to the bluff to apprehensively scan the sea. And William Steidel, playing poker with friends, ignored it all—at least at first.

What Steidel ignored at first was the telephone call that had interrupted the game, a friend calling to warn the poker players that a tsunami was coming. They had heard that one before, and they went back to their game. Then the second call came; the tsunami had arrived. "And we all hit the door at the same time. And it was just like a Laurel and Hardy picture, guys trying to get out of the room, and then it was repeated again because all the guys were parked in Frank Hammond's parking lot and they all tried to drive their cars out of the parking lot at the same time, and they couldn't get out and they had a hell of a mess."

The Snows, on their bluff, had seen the arrival of the wave, which "from a distance moved in flat, curling to shore and rising in height about a foot a second, about ten feet in all." Later, the wave—which was caused by an Alaskan earthquake—was said to have reached a height of twenty-five feet.

Meanwhile, finally extricating himself from the parking lot, Steidel made for his home on the north side of Elk Creek. After passing through the flooded center of town, he drove onto the bridge ramp to find that the bridge itself was gone. (On its way up the creek—some three hundred yards—the bridge had broken power lines; thus the blue and green lights seen by Margaret Sroufe.) Pausing on the ramp in astonishment at the absence of the bridge—one of his front wheels over the edge of the ramp—Steidel was even more astonished to see a house pass by. "It went over into the meadow and settled down, looked like someone had built it there and it hardly disturbed anything in the house. Somebody said all it moved was a coffee pot about a foot on the counter."

In addition to the washed-out bridge and the relocated house, a trailer parked in a riverside campground was struck. The owner had thought it would be safer to remain inside—until, that is, the trailer began to move, drifting in the floodwaters and finally turning on its side. Fortunately, the fire department was on hand and succeeded in getting the occupants out.

According to Steidel, except for the above, the tsunami "didn't do much damage along our coast. It just kind of hit the bank and went over the tops of the houses and that was about it." Nonetheless, Cannon Beach was reminded to a degree it had not been reminded before that the ocean was right at its door and might, at any time, come in.

CHAPTER SIX

I T IS SOMETIMES SAID when speaking of a person that such and such an event was a "turning point," that thereafter a sea change occurred. The same may be said of a place. In the case of Cannon Beach, the tsunami of 1964 might be considered such a turning point, for in the next twenty-five years the town would be transformed physically and to a large extent in character as well.

the paradoxical nature of things, it was the third ploy, intended only for locals, that in the end would draw the crowds from elsewhere, and in astounding numbers.

The first of these schemes, mainly the inspiration of Betty Dueber and Bill Steidel, was the Headless Horseman. Every Sunday, promptly at noon, the bells of the Presbyterian church would ring out and there would then appear in downtown Cannon Beach a black horse, its rider (later revealed to be Beth Dueber, Betty's daughter) draped in black from top to toe and holding in the crook of its arm its head! (Papier mache.) How many tourists this spectacle drew is uncertain, but at least it was more successful than the second scheme.

This second one also sprang from the fertile minds of Betty Dueber and Bill Steidel, along with several other miscreants. The plan was to illuminate Haystack Rock! Accordingly, the power company was persuaded to run a line to the rock and set up two huge spotlights. The first (and only) night on which the rock was lit, its great flocks of seabirds fled in terror, swooping over the town and drowning it in guano.

The third ploy was an act of playful defiance, a nose-thumbing at the previous year's tsunami. The idea was Margaret Atherton's. Richard and Margaret Atherton had settled in Cannon Beach in 1958, and until the early 1970s they enlivened the town in several significant ways. This was one of them.

Margaret's idea for putting the tsunami in its place was to hold a celebration on the beach on the day of the year's lowest tide. As part of the celebration, those interested were invited to build a sandcastle or anything else of sand they might devise. The celebration became a yearly event and it also became a contest, with prizes given for the best creations. The entry fee was a quarter, and for the quarter the entrant also got a bag of saltwater taffy. It was a homey, casual affair, mainly for the locals.

However, as might be expected, there were some among the locals who sought to "capitalize" on the event. Since the lowest tide of the year seldom fell on a weekend, it was suggested that the contest be moved to the lowest weekend tide so that people from Portland and other distant places might attend. In spite of some opposition, the change was made. The following year the crowds were so great there was hardly room for the locals on the beach.

Over the years there was a substantial increase in the crowds come to see the thirty-foot-long dragon, the enormous octopus, the mermaid of Junoesque proportions, and, of course, the sandcastles themselves. Inevitably, the crowds created problems—traffic problems, toilet problems, trash problems. These aggravations were eventually pretty well alleviated. Meanwhile, Cannon Beach had acquired its first massive tourist attraction, Sandcastle ranking with Pendleton's Round-Up and Portland's Rose Festival. As for the locals, some made money, some stayed home, some left Cannon Beach to visit friends until the event was over. Currently, an average of twenty-five thousand attend each year. The entry fee is now considerably higher, but they still throw in the taffy.

∽

Though Sandcastle became an enormous success—indeed known worldwide—it did not succeed in propitiating the gods of weather, as Margaret Atherton might have wished. In 1967, only three years after the tsunami, the town was hit by an exceptionally destructive flood. West winds of great velocity and very high tides combined to drown the town under three feet of water, fling logs through windows, and drive the occupants of the post office to a table top, from which it was necessary to rescue them by rowboat. It was also said that the flood was of such force that it moved Haystack Rock ten feet. Though that assertion is questionable, it is a fact that $125,000 in damage was done to ten businesses and that the Red Cross was called upon to open a relief center.

It was all very depressing. The earlier loss of Highway 101, the

101

double whammy of the tsunami and the flood, the logging that had supplied year-round income now almost finished, a main street of sodden, dilapidated buildings—"You know, this town is really going to pot," a local stated at the time. But she was wrong, for it was about now, in the late 1960s, that several circumstances arose that would soon turn Cannon Beach into one of the most desirable beach communities on the Pacific coast.

The first harbinger of this good fortune came when the town received some flood-disaster funds to help in the rebuilding of the place. It was decided that this might be an opportune time to develop a town plan. Accordingly, the town requested a planner from the Bureau of Municipal Research at the University of Oregon. The bureau obliged by sending up a staffer named Herbert Beals. Beals remembers the people of Cannon Beach as being particularly hospitable and helpful to him in his work. He remembers as well that they wanted a plan that would promote their economic recovery but on the other hand would not lead them in the direction of their neighbor to the north, Seaside (sometimes referred to as Sodom and sometimes as Gomorrah). Once again, the old conflict had surfaced. People had pretty much agreed on some development, but it had better not be of the kind to the north. After all, Cannon Beach, however depressed, was special!

Beals's plan was completed in 1967. This document, on file at the Cannon Beach Historical Society, is most instructive. It tells us much about the state of Cannon Beach at the time—the fact, for example, that 56 percent of the housing was "deteriorating or dilapidated." As for the future, it warned, among other things, that parking and water supply would be serious problems. It concluded with twelve recommendations, the first of which was that the town enact a "comprehensive zoning ordinance to replace the present interim one."

But it is at the very beginning of his report that Beals put his finger on the central issue.

There are indications that many visitors and summer residents return to Cannon Beach (or eventually retire there) because it retains a secluded aspect in which the natural setting predominates. Thus, among a number of persons there may be an uneasiness that the familiar, easy-going resort town they have known will disappear in the congestion, conflicts, and increased tempo of new development. A general plan for city development is one way to help achieve the maximum benefits of economic growth without sacrificing those qualities that have made Cannon Beach a desirable place in which to live or spend leisure hours . . . Essentially, a development plan can be the basis for bringing balance and harmony to the many competing forces that will be shaping Cannon Beach in the years ahead.

Many of Beals's recommendations were incorporated into the city plan of 1969. But as for the "harmony" he hoped for, that proved rather more elusive.

༄

There next occurred an event that in the nick of time saved what is indeed the specialness of Cannon Beach, as recognized by Beals: its extraordinary seascape and the beach from which that seascape is best seen and enjoyed. The central act in this high drama came about on a May morning in 1967 when, to everyone's astonishment, two helicopters landed on the beach. From one of them sprang an angry Oregon governor. The angry governor was Tom McCall.

The previous year a Cannon Beach motel owner had fenced off the beach in front of his establishment for the exclusive use of his motel guests. The state Highway Commission protested this exclusion but without success, for the motel owner had found a loophole in Governor Os West's beach bill. The 1912 bill designated only the wet sands, or seashore proper, as a public highway; it made no mention of the dry sands. Thus the motel owner was within his rights in his use of the dry sands.

This loophole prompted the Highway Commission in 1967 to

introduce a bill in the legislature to include the dry sands, fearing that otherwise all of Oregon's beaches would be lost to the public. The majority of the Republican members were opposed to the bill. Perhaps to their surprise, this earned them the fury of their governor. Thus it was that McCall appeared on the Oregon coast and brought with him a second helicopter filled with reporters and photographers. "Mad as hell," according to one of the reporters, McCall strode onto the "private" beach, posing often for the photographers. Shortly thereafter the photographs appeared in practically all the state papers. Angry letters in the thousands flayed the Republican opposition, which in short order collapsed, and the beach bill was passed. It gave the state the right to zone the dry sands as well as the wet and to outlaw any use not permitted by the Highway Commission. On signing the bill, McCall stated with considerable force that "no local, selfish interest should be permitted, through politics or otherwise, to destroy or even impair this great birthright of our people."

The next circumstance in the prospering of Cannon Beach had its origins in the distant past. Wilson Clark, an Oregon lumberman, began coming to Cannon Beach in the mid 1920s, renting a house for the summer for his wife and children, a Chinese cook, and a maid. His young son, Maurie, played on the beach, went for rides on Spaulding's rental horses, swam in the Nat, and skated at the rink—good times. Thirty years later, in the early 1960s, Maurie Clark, remembering those good times and now with children of his own, bought a house at Arch Cape.

On occasion Clark would go up the coast to his old haunts, the scenes of his boyhood in Cannon Beach. Like the locals, he found the town considerably depressed. But unlike many, he was optimistic, believing the town to be a "sleeper." Accordingly, he began to consider purchasing some lots and remembers thinking about Cannon Beach "being as close to Portland as it is and as nice as it is on the ocean, some of those lots might be worth something

The knight errant brandishing a sword is Peter Frost. He was attending a 1968 rally in Cannon Beach.

Governor Tom McCall stands outside a log barricade on May 14, 1967 in from the Surfsand Motel at Cannon Beach. The barricade was put up by the Motel owner to define the dry sand area for the guests of the motel. Such barricades brought controversy. McCall's survey resulted in a measurement formula for public-private land dispute.

someday. I'll go take a look at them next time I come through."

Shortly after this, Clark decided to build a new deck on his house at Arch Cape, for which he employed a carpenter and watercolorist named Ray Watkins. Watkins had come to Cannon Beach in 1948 and had developed a strong affection for the place—as well as some dreams for its future. It happened that by now Clark had in fact bought some Cannon Beach lots. Impressed by Watkins, Clark asked him what he would put on the lots. The story goes that Watkins sketched out on a paper napkin the kind of structure that he thought would complement the town's sensational site—a gambrel-roofed building of stone and wood with a courtyard and landscaped with natural vegetation. "I like it. Let's do it," Clark is reported to have said. And so it began. As Margaret McCluskey wrote about Watkins and Clark, "The dreamer and the dream-maker became partners in a series of building projects that would change the image of Cannon Beach."

That first building is now the south wing of Sandpiper Square. Later, what is now the north wing was added, and still later the structure that joins the two wings. Clark and Watkins went on to build or remodel nearly a dozen buildings in Cannon Beach, in the later years in association with Bill Campbell: the Mariner Market, the Coaster Theater, the Coaster Village, the Peake building (the present Cannon Beach Bookshop), the Sea Lark Apartments (low-rent units for the elderly), the U.S. Bank building with adjoining offices and shops, and the library and Chamber of Commerce buildings, among others. Much of the cost of the library and Chamber buildings was covered by Clark, his gift to the town. "Clark's investment was practical," Watkins told Margaret McCluskey, "but his primary motive was to enhance and beautify the town."

As for Watkins's part in this building program, he had, according to McCluskey, "rejected the idea of a theme town or a facsimile pioneer coastal village with false-fronted buildings." Rather, he told McCluskey, he had "purposely combined different architectural

The vision of Maurie Clark (shown above in a portrait taken in the 1970s) and Ray Watkins created Sandpiper Square which changed the look of Cannon Beach's downtown area.

styles to create a natural, aesthetically pleasing atmosphere." Different the styles may be, but nonetheless they are in harmony. This is important, for it has influenced other builders to design their structures in a style congruent with the overall Cannon Beach look. The result of the work of these two men is what many consider the most attractive small town in Oregon and one of the most pleasing on the entire Pacific coast. According to Watkins, these building projects, this sprucing up of the town, were contagious. "Enthusiasm for clean-up, patch-up, and fix-up ignited and spread like wildfire to the residential areas." But something else, too, was happening in the residential areas of the town, and it was to complete the physical transformation of Cannon Beach.

As noted in chapter 4, a good many private beach houses had been built in Cannon Beach in the 1920s, and some following World War II as well. But these were vastly outnumbered by the hundreds of rental cabins—some in the form of auto courts (with a garage between each cabin), some detached and in groups of four or five. Many of these cabins consisted of only one room and were usually rented for a week or more. Long-term rentals were customary in the 1920s and 1930s, in part because it still took the better part of a day to reach Cannon Beach from Portland, thus ruling out short-term, weekend rentals. Finally, almost all the cabins were meant for summer use only and were closed up on Labor Day, their owners often working as loggers through the winter.

In the 1950s and 1960s several changes began to occur, one of which is always with us: decay. The little cabins—flimsy from the start, having passed through forty or so coastal winters, and not always subject to much upkeep, had begun to literally fall down. At about the same time, a new form of accommodation was beginning to appear in the nation and, of course, in Cannon Beach as well: the motel.

The pioneer motel in Cannon Beach appears to have been the Bell Harbor on the northwest corner of Fifth Street and the Highway 101 Scenic Loop, the former site of the 1892 Logan House and the present site of the Ecola Creek Lodge. Built in 1946 by Perra Wilkins, the Bell Harbor was named for Wilkins's collection of bells. The establishment was considered remarkable at the time, for, as the Oregonian reported, each unit contained a radio and an electric clock!

However, the true age of the motel started in the 1950s, when they began to take the place of the often dilapidated cabins. Though a few were renovated to continue as rental cottages and a few remodeled to serve as private residences, the majority were gradually razed and replaced by motels and private houses.

Thus, over time—and not too long a time at that—Cannon Beach was physically transformed, the depressed, shacky main street evolving into a prosperous stretch of solid, generally charming structures, the outlying areas of deteriorating rental cabins gradually replaced by new motels and private houses—all in all, a case of grub to butterfly.

꙳

At about the time all this construction and remodeling was happening, various other important events were taking place in the town as well. In 1968 one side of Haystack Rock was blasted in such a fashion as to make it inaccessible. The town was tired of rescuing tourists who fancied themselves to be alpinists.

Of considerably more importance in 1968 was the annexation of Tolovana Park. At the turn of the century, Tolovana Park may have had more residents than Elk Creek, as Cannon Beach was then known. Rudolph and Emma Bartels homesteaded in the area in 1889, the Brallier brothers in 1890, and William, Edra, and Mark Warren in 1893. Other early settlers were the Andersons, Mansurs, and Settems. According to Frank Chown, many of the summer homes in Tolovana belonged to families from Astoria. At Wave Crest, the Tolovana addition platted by Frank Brallier in 1924, several Christian Science families built houses, continuing an old tradition on both the Atlantic and Pacific coasts of people of like religion locating in the same area.

As the years passed, Tolovana, though immediately adjacent to Cannon Beach—Center Street being the dividing line—developed independently, with its own post office, community club, and rather separate sense of identity. However, by the late 1960s sewer problems were such that the citizens decided annexation to Cannon Beach and its sewer system would be expeditious. Still, Tolovana Park was not about to give up its identity entirely, retaining both its name and post office. So far as Cannon Beach was concerned, its tax base was substantially increased—though so, too, were its responsibilities.

But there was another event in 1968 even more important than the annexation of Tolovana Park, for in time it would transform the character of Cannon Beach as much as Clark and Watkins and the motel entrepreneurs were transforming the look of Cannon Beach.

From the beginning, Cannon Beach had attracted artists, as well as persons of an "artistic temperament." What drew them, of course, was that Cannon Beach was beautiful, quiet, and affordable—those conditions that almost all artists require. Who knows, Herbert Logan in the light of his silver candlesticks may have sketched out from memory his ancestral home. Who knows, Jimmy the Tough may have longed for a paint box rather than his rod and net. But a true flocking of artists to Cannon Beach had to wait upon the initiative of Richard Atherton, husband of the woman responsible for Sandcastle, he himself a real estate agent, promoter, and above all a man with lots of ideas. Atherton was determined to make Cannon Beach an arts center. His first effort was not particularly successful. He hired a woman from California to give painting lessons, providing her with a generous salary as well as a studio in a building he owned. According to one local, "All she did was invite herself out to dinner at people's houses and paint for personal sale." Somewhat more successfully, Atherton brought down an aeronautical engineer from Seattle to teach kite flying.

Atherton persisted, and in 1968, with some local support and in particular with help from Stan Glarum of Lewis and Clark College's music department and from Fred Kline of Portland State University's art department, the Haystack Summer Arts program was born. Meeting in the elementary school, the program offered instruction in the graphic arts, music, writing, theater, and environmental studies. On Friday evenings, teachers and students presented a free program for the town. There was also a weekly picnic on the beach, sometimes called the "soggy doggy" because the rain so often dampened the hot dog buns.

Haystack's first years were touch and go, but Atherton's determination, more support from the town (particularly in the person of Dave Firebaugh), and the continued cooperation of the participating institutions put the program on a firm and lasting foundation. Its influence was reflected three years after its founding by an *Oregonian* article that called Cannon Beach "as much an artist colony as Sausalito or Greenwich Village" and noted its "11 art shops"—among them Evelyn Georges's White Bird Gallery, one of the first galleries in Cannon Beach and now the oldest gallery on the Oregon coast.

The *Oregonian*'s comparison of Cannon Beach with Sausalito and Greenwich Village is rather an exaggeration but there is no doubt that Haystack had, and continues to have, a profound impact on the character of the town. As Lucille Houston, a former mayor, has said, "I think that [Haystack] was probably the most significant thing that happened to the city of Cannon Beach to make it the kind of city it is." At about the same time as the influx of artists in the late 1960s and the 1970s, there was an influx of a related kind. Perhaps the term "dropout" will serve as well as any other. These were people who, like the artists, wanted a place that was beautiful, quiet, and affordable, people who had given up on "winning," on "making it," people

113

interested in being rather than in acting. The coast has, of course, always attracted such people, but with the counterculture of the 1960s their numbers greatly increased. In the case of Cannon Beach, some just drifted through; but others stayed, or went away and came back. And some, like the artists, made important contributions to the town and helped to permanently alter its character.

Haystack was not Richard Atherton's only project. In the following year, 1969, he brought to Cannon Beach the Portland State University Players, thus inaugurating summer theater in the town—now expanded to other seasons as well.

The PSU players were not, however, the town's first thespians. They had been preceded in the early 1960s by the Steidel Players, a group of locals who met in the Commercial Club's Quonset hut to put on lip-synch revues featuring songs from the popular musicals of the time. It is said that the costuming and synchronization were flawless. But the productions are remembered in particular for being purely local, put on by the motel and cabin operators, restaurant proprietors and cooks, the variety-store owner with all nine of her children, the butcher, the baker, the gas pumper—people in a little place getting together to entertain one another on winter nights.

Though the passing of the Steidel Players was noted with regret, the arrival of Atherton's theater was greeted with enthusiasm, for not only had Atherton brought the Portland players to Cannon Beach, he had also provided them and the town with an actual theater. Several years before, he had bought the by then ramshackle skating rink. In 1968 he and a number of volunteers began the conversion of the old building into the Coaster Theater, hurrying to ready it for the PSU Players first season in 1969. Their season was a great success—troubled only by the city council's concern for the players' morality. Though the actors were chaperoned in quarters on the theater's second floor, some council members suspected

114

"wicked" goings-on. According to Janet Rekate, a frequent second-floor visitor, "the wickedest thing they were doing up there was making popcorn and eating it with apples."

Popcorn and apples. A gentle ending to a turbulent and momentous decade: the tsunami, the flood, Sandcastle and Haystack, the inclusion of Tolovana, a city plan, and, finally, the beginnings of a town that was different in both look and character. Change was gaining momentum, faster and faster, and in its speeding flow the old Cannon Beach would soon be lost.

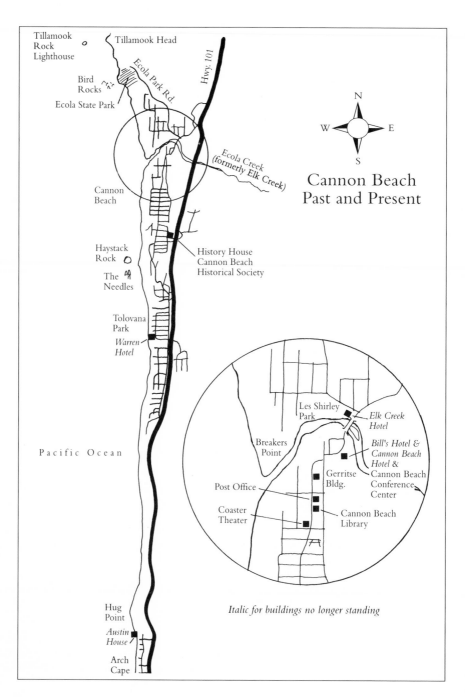

Tillamook Rock Lighthouse

Tillamook Head

Bird Rocks

Ecola Park Rd.

Hwy. 101

Ecola State Park

Ecola Creek (formerly Elk Creek)

Cannon Beach

Cannon Beach Past and Present

History House Cannon Beach Historical Society

Haystack Rock

The Needles

Tolovana Park

Warren Hotel

Les Shirley Park

Elk Creek Hotel

Breakers Point

Bill's Hotel & Cannon Beach Hotel & Cannon Beach Conference Center

Gerritse Bldg.

Post Office

Pacific Ocean

Coaster Theater

Cannon Beach Library

Hug Point

Austin House

Arch Cape

Italic for buildings no longer standing

116

CHAPTER SEVEN

NOTHING SYMBOLIZED THE PASSING of the old Cannon Beach more than two events that occurred at the beginning of the next decade. In 1971 the Warren Hotel and the Cannon Beach Hotel (formerly Bill's), built in 1911 and 1904, were demolished. More than just the physical structures went with the wrecking ball. A way of life went, too. In the smart new motels and condominiums that were to take the place of the old hotels, there was no common room unless one wished to count the office—hardly an equivalent to the big, paneled, beam-ceilinged lounges of the old hotels, where in the evenings guests would rock in wicker chairs before the fire, chatting, getting to know each other, telling tales. The click of knitting needles, someone in a corner with a book, children sprawled on the carpet, frowning over checkers.

In the motel and condo offices there was usually a vending machine and, most importantly, an ice machine at the end of each corridor; some even housed restaurants as well. But even the latter were no equivalent to the dining rooms of the two old hotels. For one thing, both these hotels were "American plan," which meant that meals were included in the room charge. And certainly none of the new restaurants offered the equivalent of Mrs. Osburn's blackberry pie drenched in the rich cream of the hotel cow, or the big bowls of mussels placed gratis on all the tables at the Warren—and refilled, too, when empty.

Of course, the old hotels had their problems. Construction-wise, they were not all that tight, sand drifting in under the doors, around the windows. Also, guests were subjected to what now would be considered the intolerable indignity of sharing "the facility" at the end of the hall. Finally, there was the problem of the thin lath walls of the bedrooms and all the noise that penetrated—the couple in the next room, for example, and the heavy, pounding surf. Though many people said the sound of the surf (if not the couple in the next room) gave them an especially sound night's sleep.

Whatever, by the end of 1971 the old buildings were gone—and for that matter, so were most of the people who over the years had rocked before the fires and slept in the old surf-sounding rooms. In the case of the Cannon Beach Hotel, the Conference Center decided that the building no longer served its purposes, and local opposition to its razing soon petered out. Likewise the Warren Hotel. It, too, served in its later years as a Christian conference center; when investors decided in 1971 to replace it with condominiums the protest was again not sustained.

A third protest also arose in 1971, provoked by a planned condo-

Breakers Point, 1996.

*A circa 1910 view of the site that would later be
known as Breakers Point.*

minium development called Breakers Point: 175 units in the dune lands just north of Elk Creek's entry to the sea. This protest, however, did not fizzle out, but would continue at a furious boil for the next eight years. During that time the controversy would divide the community over the issue of growth. This had happened often in the past, but never for so long, never with such acrimony as now. Now, too, for the first time, the issue of ecology would be joined to that of growth.

ᔓ

Fortunately, the bitter, almost decade-long controversy over Breakers Point was tempered somewhat by several "developments" of a happier kind. In 1972 Maurie Clark purchased Atherton's skating rink-turned-theater and remodeled it into a first-class facility. In addition to the PSU Players, the Coaster Theater would be used by the Clackamas Community College Players and in time by the Mark Allen Players, among others. In 1973 it became home for the centerpiece play of Cannon Beach's annual Dickens Christmas Festival (well-attended in part because during this period of gas shortages Cannon Beach became known as a place one could reach on one tank of fuel). Later, the Oregon Coast Performing Arts Society brought a number of performances to its stage. The Coaster was extensively used for concerts, especially those presented by the North Coast Chamber Orchestra. According to Stephen Diehl, theater director at the Coaster, "the partnership with Clark and the Coaster Theater has played a major role in the concept of Cannon Beach being known as an arts community." Such, of course, was Clark's desire. He hoped, too, that the Coaster would serve as a community center, and it indeed did for a time.

ᔓ

Beginning in about the middle of the decade, there were other happy developments. Two of these concerned flowing water—the

120

Right: In 1976, the spirit that loves books found a beautiful home in the Cannon Beach Library.

Below: Coaster Theater.

121

water in the pipes and the water in the creek. In the first case, the town took over the operation of the water system from the Firebaughs' private company. In the second, the creek at long last was given back the name by which Captain Clark had called it: Ecola.

Other civic accomplishments during this time included the opening of a children's day-care center in 1975 and the start of a recycling program, one of the first and most successful in the state. In the following year the town was provided with its first medical clinic, and at Dick Atherton's urging Victoria Hawkins founded the *Cannon Beach Gazette*, a biweekly paper that is still publishing.

The most important of these mid-decade events, however, was the culmination of nearly fifty years of effort. It was in 1927 that what came to be called the Cannon Beach Library and Women's Club was founded to provide the town with a good library. Having started in rented space and later acquiring a make-do cottage, now, at last, in 1976, the club was able to design and construct its own building—one of the most attractive small libraries in the state.

As noted earlier, these happy developments of the 1970s were only a partial distraction from the controversy that raged over that other development, Breakers Point. Favoring the project for economic reasons were the mayor and city council. Opposed was a coalition of nearly forty artists, environmentalists, and others who objected to the project's density—175 units on less than seven acres—and to the fact that a portion of the development would occupy a foredune and thus, it was charged, do environmental damage.

The controversy soon went to the courts. First the attorney general, representing the Highway Commission, claimed that the public had a recreational easement over a portion of the site. Next the 1,000 Friends of Oregon sued the city, citing density and ecological problems. At the same time the Land Conservation and Development Commission, which was now in operation, brought suit on the basis of a geological report that the foredune was unstable and thus not suitable for building.

The controversy, as controversies are wont to do, flared tempers and sometimes provoked outbursts of a rather extreme nature. To some outsiders, these social fireworks appeared more comic than serious. For example, a resident of Arch Cape, at a safe remove from the battlefield, wrote to the *Cannon Beach Gazette* in December of 1976:

> The pleasures of living in this area of the coast are manifold ... But by far the most enjoyable and amusing aspect of life here is the frequent entertainment provided at no charge by the citizens of Cannon Beach who, out of their concern for intellectual stimulation of the populace, perform the on-going comedy/drama titled 'Municipal Politics' ... the townspeople play their parts with sincerity, passion and self-indulgence ... Encouraged by the apparent fact that participation required nothing in the way of logic, rational intelligence, or even an orderly mind, I enter into the spirit of the proceedings by using an inordinate number of words to say nothing, but hopefully in an inflammatory manner.

Few in Cannon Beach saw any humor in the situation, especially when, a month after the *Gazette* letter, someone poured sugar into the gas tank of a tractor clearing at the site.

To everyone's relief, the controversy was finally settled by compromise in 1978. The developers withdrew from the foredune and reduced the number of units from 175 to 71. The following year the groundbreaking took place, followed by a champagne lunch attended by the proponents and even some former opponents. There was peace at last—though it may have been the kind of peace that follows from exhaustion.

The Land Conservation and Development Commission appeared in Cannon Beach not only as a litigant in the Breakers Point controversy, but in another sense as well, for its charge to provide statewide land-use planning goals required that every county and municipality prepare a comprehensive plan. Cannon Beach began work on its plan (actually a revision of its 1969 plan) in early 1977, in the midst of the Breakers Point controversy—an issue that probably affected the new plan.

In order to help determine what kind of plan and thus what kind of town people wanted, 750 questionnaires were distributed to both full-time and part-time residents. Three hundred and sixty-one, or 48 percent, were completed, an exceptionally high return. The answers to the questions made it very clear what the majority of respondents desired. Sixty-eight percent agreed with the characterization of Cannon Beach as "a small, quiet beach town that should essentially remain that way . . . and should concentrate on increasing the quality of life in the city rather than increasing the numbers of people who come here." Only 11 percent believed that the town "should make greater efforts to attract tourism and commercial development"—though one respondent thought that "more tourism might attract some normal people for a change."

Other responses were highly indicative as well: a majority wanted the streets left as they were—any that were narrow and graveled should be neither widened nor paved; no more land set aside for motels; and design review for all buildings "to insure that construction is attractive and in keeping with the town's character." However, one of the 9 percent opposed to any design review thought otherwise. "Maybe I don't like the town's character and I want to be my own individual. I think you have to go to city hall now to flush the toilet."

In general, the message was very clear; and it was remembered, too, when the Planning Commission, together with mainly business interests, began working on the downtown portion of the plan. Finished in September of 1977, the plan had as its central provision, embodied in item 2, an attempt to balance the competing interests of business and residents: "The City, through its planning and zoning policies, should maintain the downtown area as a place for residents *and* tourists, and make efforts to insure that the promotion of the tourist industry does not sacrifice those small town amenities that are important to townspeople, especially scale."

The plan went on to call for "a compact town center" of small-scale businesses, which would be encouraged to provide "benches, plantings and open space" and which would be signed "in keeping with present trends," i.e., signs of a fairly rustic appearance *sans* neon. The plan also called for "low cost housing for the elderly and for people who work in downtown businesses." Finally, it tackled the growing problem of parking by recommending a municipal parking lot, and in fact such a lot, accommodating a hundred cars, was constructed the following year. These and other provisions of the plan, along with the earlier questionnaire results, make it clear that the influx of artists and others of like interests had begun to have a distinct influence on the governance of the town and its plans for the future.

$$\backsim$$

There are, however, certain institutions, associations, and commonalities that no amount of planning can provide. The reason is that they are random, arising out of happenstance, fortuitous flukes, as it were. In Cannon Beach there were two such institutions. Sadly, they passed at the end of the 1970s, as the two old hotels had passed at the decade's beginning. One was a gas station, the other a small, down-at-the-heels cafe.

By the time of his retirement in 1979, Les Ordway had operated the Chevron gas station for forty-one years. But the number of years he spent there was only part of the station's significance. More important were the dozens of Cannon Beach boys who worked in the station during those forty-one years. "It was," said George Shields, "a school for boys," by which he meant that Ordway taught the boys more than just how to tinker a motor into purring like a

Left and above: *These 1975 photos show an active
Cannon Beach kite shop.*

Below: *Still active twenty years later, this 1996 photo shows the
growth of businesses fronting the kite shop.*

127

kitten. He also taught them the importance of punctuality, diligence, civility, and helpfulness. Many men now old, some retired from positions of considerable importance, remember with gratitude the lessons learned from Les Ordway over at the gas station.

The other institution that no planner or consultant could have "programmed," was the cafe called the Round Table which was opened by Evie and Win Boothby in 1961 in the "post office building." It was so named because the cafe consisted mainly of a round table eight feet in diameter and surrounded by twelve stools.

The Round Table gained popularity for several reasons. The Boothbys were an affable couple and good cooks to boot. Unlikely as it may seem from its name, Win Boothby's sauerkraut custard pie even challenged the reputation of Mrs. Osburn's cream-drenched blackberry pie at Bill's Hotel. The Round Table was also a convenient place to stop in for coffee, and perhaps a piece of the sauerkraut pie, either before or after the 9 AM mail was ready next door at the post office. Finally, there was no better source of local news than the Round Table. Though one malcontent called it a "gossipy place," this was denied by its patrons. "People told things," said one, "but nobody ever tried to hurt anybody."

In January of 1978, in anticipation of the Boothbys' retirement, the *Cannon Beach Gazette* wrote: "A landmark in Cannon Beach, the Round Table is where patrons sit and share the events of the day; work crossword puzzles, argue politics, local and national; discourse on literature, arts and sports; maybe even write a letter; share a chuckle found in their morning mail or read a book . . . The atmosphere is as casual and warm as a family gathering."

With the departure of the Boothbys in February of 1978, the Round Table closed, but reopened a few months later under new management. In 1981, when the decision was made to build a new post office, the old building was razed and the Round Table closed for good. Nothing in the town ever replaced it. Surely it was for that reason that the old table itself was finally saved and stored at the Chamber of Commerce—a reminder of the camaraderie of another time.

〜

"The camaraderie of another time." So it was remembered. Janet Rekate, who settled in Cannon Beach in 1963, speaks of "the intimacy that people used to have with one another." Lucille Houston, who came in 1972, recalls that "everybody knew everybody. People were responsible for one another." Other old-timers have similar memories of the town before its fairly stable population of about five hundred began to increase, more than doubling by the 1980s. The increase not simply quantitative, had a qualitative effect as well. The camaraderie so aptly symbolized by the Round Table had been mainly a reflection of the town's small size. One cannot be companionable with a crowd.

So as the town came into the late 1970s and 1980s, the old intimacy began to pass, and it was missed by those who had once known it. But there was another change, too—one not so much regretted as actively opposed, at least by some. This was the enormous increase in the number of tourists that occurred in these years.

Here again, the change was not simply quantitative but also qualitative, for the tourists were a very different breed from the earlier "summer people." The latter, according to George Shields, not only "stayed all summer but became a part of the community and understood local customs." When they left on Labor Day, there was regret—regret on the part of the local children at the departure of their summer playmates, regret on the part of the local merchants at the departure of their customers. But there was also a certain relief; now the town could return to "normal," to the isolation, quietness, and peace of the coastal winter. There was a time in the 1960s when Dick Atherton used to signify the Labor Day exodus by shooting off his toy cannon down the length of Hemlock Street.

129

No more. For not only were there more tourists coming for shorter stays, but the tourists were also now coming year-round. The spreading knowledge that some of the best coast weather was in the autumn, the building of motels for winter use in contrast to the old summer-only tourist cabins, the growing popularity of storm and whale watching, the increasing number of urban-caliber restaurants, more disposable income—whatever the reasons, the locals saw their town flooded with the ever-coming, ever-increasing, ever-changing crowds and which, furthermore, in contrast with the past, were crowds of . . . strangers.

Another change that tended to alienate many of the locals from the tourists was a certain kind of change in the physical town. For most of its history, Cannon Beach had been like any other small town in its commercial establishments: a grocery or two, a butcher shop, perhaps a bakery, a gas station and garage, a tavern, a variety store, a lumberyard, a mom-and-pop cafe. The variety store would have carried the few tourist items then offered: postcards, starfish and sand dollars, a marine scene painted on a rock, clam shovels, sunglasses and sun hats, and, for children, the gaily painted little buckets and spades for playing in the sand.

With the increase in tourism, there were significant additions. In the mid-1970s the *Oregonian* reported that in Cannon Beach "more than 33 shops opened last year!" The majority of these establish-ments—gift shops, art galleries, restaurants—served not the locals but the tourists, and thus to the residents were in a sense extraneous, in a sense not *theirs*. At about the same time, these local feelings were aggravated when the Chamber of Commerce reported that some tourists complained of the "irregular hours" kept by Cannon Beach businesses. The implication that local proprietors should shape up was met with considerable indignation. Irregular hours were the norm in most coastal communities. For some, at least, that was the attraction of operating a business at the coast: one could open and close when one damn well pleased.

~

In view of all these changes, the results of the comprehensive plan's 1977 questionnaire are understandable—the desire for "a small, quiet beach town" that would "concentrate on increasing the quality of life . . . rather than increasing the numbers of people who come here." In part it was nostalgia for the smaller Cannon Beach of the past, where "everybody knew everybody," including the summer people. In part it was because of a tourist population that was now on average about ten times the size of the local population. This made the locals feel that they had lost their town, that it had been taken over by tourists—and tourists who, like sailors in a port, took their pleasures and then moved on . . . leaving some problems behind.

There was, of course, the other side; as one local merchant said at the time, "I made a significant investment in this place. Without the tourists I'll go under." It was the old story, the old conflict, but now more bitter than ever before. In the next decade it would grow still more bitter. On the other hand, there were those who called for understanding, and they were successful to some extent—all, perhaps, that could be expected.

CHAPTER EIGHT

THE 1980s BEGAN WITH A CHALLENGE to those who wished to keep the "village look" of Cannon Beach. A local motel owner asked the city's approval for the construction of a seven-story, stepped-back hotel reminiscent in design of those at Waikiki. The city council unanimously denied the request. The developer later submitted a radically revised proposal in harmony with the town's scale and its rather huddled profile. The city approved.

It was at about this time as well that the city was confronted with an issue that was a matter less of appearance than of content, as it were—tourists occupying the town's rental units. For some time, residents had complained that more and more houses in their neighborhoods were being rented by the night in the same fashion as motels.

Private houses had traditionally been rented out in the summer in Cannon Beach, but for at least a week, usually for two weeks, often for the month, and commonly to families who returned to the same house at the same time year after year—in other words, quasi-neighbors. This was very different from the one-or two-night stays by strangers. Another change was that in the past, house owners in general rented only enough to help with the taxes and upkeep, reserving the houses for themselves the rest of the time. Now, more and more houses were owned by persons who used them for rentals only, the houses being simply investments. This hardly made such people "neighbors," with all that that implies.

The full-time residents also complained that the houses were too often rented, or anyway occupied, by too many people. This resulted in lots of cars and parking problems—especially when the renters threw a party, which was not uncommon. And, of course, parties tend to be noisy. It was all too much. Finally, in 1982, the city took action, prohibiting rentals of less than two weeks. This left some people decidedly unhappy.

The following year another measure was passed (though this time by initiative) that required proprietors of all tourist accommodations to assess a room tax payable to the city. The rationale lay in the comment of a citizen who in her complaint no doubt represented many others: "I get tired of my taxes going higher to give services to all the tourists."

These measures—the prohibition on short-term rentals and the room tax—as well as other squabbles led to such bad feeling that two of the town's cooler heads were impelled to write letters to the *Gazette* calling for reconciliation. One letter noted "a steady and insidious erosion of community spirit," adding that when "there were disagreements in the past, they tended to be viewed with a sense of humor rather than antagonism." The other letter lamented that the "approach to our problems is so often divisive or personally antagonistic that it is seriously endangering the workings of this city. It is time that something be done."

Oil on troubled waters. But the oil soon dispersed, the waters troubled once again. In response to the Chamber's call for more year-round tourism, one citizen maintained, in a letter to the *Gazette*, that "many people do not think that Cannon Beach needs boosters . . . that increased efforts to accommodate the tourist trade have taken much away that made the town a good place to live."

City officials attempted to mediate, to bring fairness to both sides of the issue. "How do we retain a this-is-our-home atmosphere and yet not take away tourists who contribute to the economic health of many?" said Mayor Lucille Houston at a 1985 council meeting. And Councilman Herbert Schwab reminded people of reality: "Much as we may look back with understandable nostalgia to the time when Cannon Beach was a laid-back, pristine coastal village, we can't turn back the clock. Today Cannon Beach is a booming tourist town." This did not mean that Schwab was indifferent to the rights of the town's residential community, for in 1987 he was the principal founder of the Homeowners Association as a counterforce to tourist interests. Focusing in particular on out-of-town beach-house owners, who tended to be overlooked, the association had nearly a thousand members by 1988.

Conflicts between the Homeowners Association and the Chamber of Commerce were, of course, inevitable, and they were heightened by the 1988 Sandcastle—which brought thirty thousand tourists to the town at a time when its population was twelve hundred. It was about now, too, that a bumper sticker appeared that read "Welcome to the Cannon Beach Mall, formerly a residential community."

Back and forth the controversy swung. "A select few," a merchant wrote to the *Gazette*, "may wish that visitors were not able to enter town . . . but the rest of us are trying to make a living and we need visitors to survive." On the other hand, when the Chamber of Commerce demanded more money from the city's room tax in order to promote more tourism, a city councilor thundered back that the city needed the funds to take care of the problems that the promotion of tourism caused.

And so it went, each side winning a few and losing a few. In 1987, for example, the prohibition against short-term house rentals was rescinded, since it was found impossible to fully enforce. (In the following decade the ordinance would be reinstated.) On the other hand, the Chamber's 1989 attempt to rezone the downtown to permit greater density by decreasing on-site parking was defeated.

In the end, the conflict between the growth and anti-growth factions, however rancorous in its expression, did produce a kind of balance—though the extremes of the two factions, both then and now, would probably disagree with that assessment. There were those, however, who might well have endorsed the statement of Boyd Gibbons, a former Deputy Secretary of the Interior: "The answer to bad development is not STOP. The answer to bad development is good development." Some, perhaps many, would argue that Cannon Beach has chosen that latter answer.

It might seem from the foregoing that the town, both officially and otherwise, spent much of its time in squabbles over the issue of growth. In fact, many issues arose in the 1980s that were settled cooperatively and with benefit to all.

One of these was the completion in 1980 of the comprehensive plan, as called for by the Land Conservation and Development Commission. No one was entirely satisfied with all its provisions, but nonetheless it was viewed in general as an acceptable compromise. Cannon Beach also gained the distinction of being the first municipality in the state to submit its plan to the commission.

Another achievement in 1980 was the inauguration of a plan to update a facility no town can do without, growth or no growth: a good sewer system. The Cannon Beach system was unable to meet the standards imposed by the federal Clean Water Act of 1972. A Sewer Advisory Board under the inspired direction of a local innkeeper, Donald Thompson, sought an alternative to the customary, and costly, high-tech systems. Following four years of research and negotiation with various public agencies, the board, using local wetlands, succeeded by 1984 in creating one of the nation's first ecologically interactive sewage-treatment facilities.

It was in 1984 as well that a basic change was made in the town's governance. Overwhelmed by the issues engendered by growth, the mayor and the council, who served part-time and without pay, proposed to the electorate that the city charter be amended to provide for a city manager. The voters agreed, much to the relief of the council and Her Honor.

Another achievement of that year was an acquisition engineered by Councilman Herbert Schwab. Some years before, the state had purchased a plot of land on the "Canadian side," as the area north of the creek was sometimes called, with the intention of laying out a park. When time passed and no park appeared, Schwab persuaded the state to deed the property to the town. It happened that the American Legion owned a portion of the adjacent land and this, too, was given to the town, though with the provision that the proposed park be named for Les Shirley, a prominent Legion member and good citizen. Before the time of paid street cleaners, it had been Shirley's custom to patrol the town with a barrel on wheels picking up litter. The town also succeeded in having the park marked as one of Lewis and Clark's six officially designated campsites in Oregon.

Another success in these middle years of the decade occurred in 1985, when the city developed policies on cars and parking both in the town and on the beach. With the increase in tourism, both areas had become problems. Now, land was purchased adjacent to the main street for a free public parking lot, and other land was bought later for the same purpose.

As for the beach, the 1985 policy was the culmination of a long history of increasing regulation, though the latter was much complicated and to some extent retarded by the fact that no coastal town has authority over its beach except as specifically permitted by the state parks department. Beginning in 1950, driving was restricted to certain areas at certain times of the year; but enforcement was sporadic, to say the least. Attempts to increase enforcement and restrictions were met by several arguments: the town needed the parking space; the disabled needed easy access; wood burners needed the driftwood; dory owners needed a launching area; and, the most frequent argument of all, "My daddy always drove on the beach." After a multitude of hearings, the 1985 ordinance was finally enacted. All driving was now prohibited except by special permit. Likewise, parking on the beach was entirely prohibited except during Sandcastle and for special-permit holders such as the disabled and those launching dory boats.

One of the town's major concerns in the following years was the updating of the 1980 comprehensive plan, as required by the Land Conservation and Development Commission. The plan finally agreed upon in 1988 recognized that the town center could no longer accommodate more people and buildings, and thus the plan included inducements for development in "mid-town," i.e., in the vicinity of Hemlock and Sunset. The plan focused as well on the "city's village atmosphere" (an interesting juxtaposition) and strongly emphasized such matters as protection of the town's natural environment, design standards for construction, and encouragement of the visual and performing arts. (In time the design-review functions of the Planning Commission, which were extensive, were taken over by a separate design-review board.)

Now, too, the city concerned itself with two events that might occur in the future, neither welcome. One was another tsunami, in the face of which Cannon Beach would be defenseless. Accordingly, when the fire horn rusted out in 1988, it was decided, with much prompting by Alfred Aya, to combine its replacement with a tsunami warning system called COWS (Community Warning System)— appropriately named, since the test alarm resembles the lowing of a cow. It was hoped it would provide sufficient time for evacuation.

Then there was the matter of the hills to the east, which form the town's backdrop. Would they turn from forest green to clear-cut brown? In 1987 the city began discussions with the timber owners, discussions that have continued and that seek agreements limiting, so far as possible, scenic degradation of the hills.

There were also the simple housekeeping tasks that any city government must perform: street cleaning, a new public restroom, upgrading the tennis courts, increasing the police force, paving the parking lot, building a bandstand. One problem, the matter of house numbers, had bedeviled the city since the founding of the volunteer fire department in 1946. The specific location of a fire was, of course, crucial to the firefighters, but many Cannon Beach residents somehow never got around to putting up their house numbers. The city finally lost patience (after forty-one years) and instituted a fifty-dollar fine for slackers. One council member was not entirely approving, reflecting perhaps the coastal predisposition to a gentle anarchism: "Seems like a pretty stiff penalty in a country where we say 'Let freedom ring.'"

Meanwhile, the city continued to make policy to deal with more substantial issues. One of these concerned affordable housing for the increasing numbers of workers that the increasing numbers of tourists had brought to the town. Many of these workers, on minimum wage or only slightly more, could not afford the high Cannon Beach rents, especially in the summer. In an effort to solve this problem, the city did itself proud by creating a Cannon Beach Community Development

Community Hall in the Cannon Beach Visitor Information Center.
The beautiful and whimsical artistic contributions throughout the hall make it a
warm and welcoming place.

The Gerritse Building. A butcher shop and library in it's previous lives,
it is now the home to the White Bird Gallery.

Above: Hemlock Street on a wet January day in 1996.

Right: A further stroll along Hemlock Street, the city still wearing its Christmas finery.

Below: A Cannon Beach Post Office that would amaze former mail carrier Mary Gerritse with its grandeur.

141

Corporation, which enabled it to apply for federal funds for affordable housing. Several years later, thirty-six units of such housing were constructed.

In the private sector, there were some interesting and useful developments as well. A Cannon Beach Historical Society had been founded in 1969, but soon languished. According to one commentator, its "meetings were very random and funding even more so." The same could have been said when the society was revived in 1983; it again quickly expired. But hope springs eternal in the historically inclined heart, and in 1988 a group of former members and others mounted a first-class exhibit on the history of Cannon Beach in the Clatsop County Historical Society's Heritage Museum in Astoria. In 1990 the Cannon Beach Society, this Lazarus of institutions, was revived once again—but this time it was placed on firm ground, unlike the shifting sands into which it had disappeared in the past. (See appendix 2 for information on the Cannon Beach Historical Society.)

Another interesting development was the beginning of the Haystack Rock Awareness Program in 1983. The inspiration of Neal and Karen Maine, its purpose was to instruct the public in the sea life associated with Haystack Rock—the starfish and crabs, the chitons, the limpets and mollusks, the tufted puffins. The method was simple: a blackboard was set up at the rock announcing the times of the educational talks. That first summer there were only three talks. In time, and with the help of groups like the Puffin Club, the talks were increased to thirty a season, the times posted in motels and other public places. In 1989 the program's efforts to protect the rock's sea life were enhanced when Haystack was designated a Marine Garden by the U.S. Fish and Wildlife Service.

In 1986 another organization appeared in Cannon Beach whose purpose, at least in part, was also educational. The principal purpose of the Cannon Beach Arts Association, however, was to "revitalize the presence of the arts." The *Gazette* echoed this hope in its comment on the new organization: "Cannon Beach may be on the verge of a revitalization of its former image as an art colony." The wording of both these statements is interesting. The need to "revitalize" the arts? Cannon Beach's "former image as an art colony?" What had happened?

As noted earlier, artists were originally drawn to Cannon Beach because it was beautiful, affordable, and quiet. It was still beautiful, but it was no longer quiet; nor could most artists afford the rents, let alone the house prices. The association attempted to alleviate those problems in several ways. With the help of Maurie Clark, it provided a gallery for local artists in Sandpiper Square where the artists received a larger percentage from sales of their work than in commercial galleries. In addition, it provided small grants to artists. The association also broadened its programs to include summer concerts, literary readings, and artists in the schools. The association became and remains today one of Cannon Beach's most important institutions.

∽

The most auspicious event to end the decade of the eighties was the completion of the new Chamber of Commerce building. A handsome structure in the "Cannon Beach style," it included offices, a visitors' information center, and a community hall. And it was "community" that had created the building—a joint effort of those occasional adversaries, the Chamber, City Hall, and the town's artists, a reassuring example of the cooperation that communities of diverse interests sometimes strive for and sometimes achieve.

One of the last events of 1990 to be held in the new community hall was a birthday party for ninety-year-old Frank Hammond, a beloved Cannon Beach sign painter. For old times' sake and because it had occupied Frank's favorite hangout, the round table was hauled out, and people sat around it talking of the past. So far as is known, however, there was no talk of that other "90," nor was there any talk of it at the ball that ended the year at the Coaster Theater. Forgotten.

**WELCOME TO HAYSTACK ROCK
MARINE
OBSERVATION AREA**

All living things, plant and animal, are protected;
collection is not allowed in an area within 300 meters
of Haystack Rock. You are encouraged to look at
these residents of Haystack Rock, but please take
only pictures and leave only footprints in the sand.

Remember, every place you walk there is probably a
living thing underfoot, especially on the slippery
rocks that are underwater most of the time. Please
use care and caution when exploring tidepools.

Because Haystack Rock is a fragile bird nesting area,
climbing on the rock above the high tide line is not
allowed. Please respect the restricted area signs.

Haystack Rock Awareness Program

**HAYSTACK ROCK
AWARENESS PROGRAM TODAY**

144

Left: Haystack Rock Awareness program sign.

Above: Digging in the sand at Cannon Beach.

Bottom left: Participants in Haystack Rock Awareness program looking at and returning animals to tidepools.

Following pages: Winter storm at Cannon Beach.

145

But ghosts, they say, have long memories, and who knows but that there among the whirling dancers there were not some other dancers, too (albeit invisible, as is often the way with ghosts), who, remembering, had come to celebrate that other "90"—1890, the year the road was put through to Elk Creek, the beginnings of the place today called Cannon Beach—and now, a hundred years later, its centenary; that's what they had come to celebrate!

Certainly Mary Gerritse and John, her sailor husband, would have been there. (With Prince, Mary's horse, tethered outside, perhaps? After all, if there are human ghosts, why not ghosts of horses, especially a horse like Prince?) Then the Austins from the old hotel below Hug Point, known for its shell path to the beach, its hearty chowders, and organ-playing of an evening. Also Jimmy the Tough, the fisherman of Jockey Cap—a good dancer, too, being Irish. But the most elegant dancer, of course, would have been Herbert Logan, he of the silver candlesticks and the Chinese butler. Then his competitor, Lester Bill, who had had the wit to salvage those logs from the beach for his hotel. The other hotel people would have been there, too—the Warrens of Alaska and Tolovana. And speaking of the Warrens, Rudolph Bartels, who used to wade the creek with the candy and booze held high, wondered why his son had not built the Coaster a fireplace like the one he'd built at the Warrens' place, a fine, big fireplace where on a winter's night the dancers might stand to warm their backsides. Also, and somewhat to the surprise of the others, irascible Major Gillespie of Terrible Tilly put in an appearance together with poor Mr. Wheeler, his much-abused assistant. Fortunately, ghosts take up no space, or there never would have been room on the floor for all those Portland families from the head; Flanders, Glisan, Minott, and Lewis. Only one figure was conspicuously absent from this reunion: Governor Os West. But apparently even his ghost did not approve of dancing.

What, one wonders, did they all think of Cannon Beach, now, a hundred years later? Certainly they would have missed the old hotels:

the Logan House, Bill's, the Warrens', the Austin House. Such comfortable places. Why gone? And the curious structures that had taken their place? "Nothing but barracks," Major Gillespie might have barked. Also, Jimmy the Tough wondered where all the crabs and clams had gone—fish, too, for that matter, and you had to buy permission to catch them and then hardly enough for a really good feed! One thing they all agreed on: the place seemed terribly crowded, and it was especially strange that the people often didn't seem to know each other. But what astonished them most of all was the fact that the ball was due to end at 1:00 AM! What was wrong? Were the people tired? Didn't they like to dance? As Mary reminded everyone, in their day the balls went on till dawn—after which they started on the day's chores.

On the other hand, they all agreed that there had been some improvements. For one thing, the place was no longer a swamp, which in their time it had been for much of the year. And the roads! Mary couldn't find any of the trails she and Prince had used. And Rudolph Bartels had good reason to be pleased by the bridge across the creek. One and all they praised the look of the town: the pretty buildings, the flowers, the little courtyards, charming. There was another change, too, that delighted them all—well, almost all. The south side of the head had been made into a park. Only Lester Bill and Herbert Logan lamented that it was not the site of a resort hotel. This set them all to arguing until Governor West—who had finally deigned to appear, since the dancing was almost over—stamped his foot, and they all shut up.

It was then that Mary pointed out to the others what had not changed: Tilly's Rock, Haystack, Chapman Point, Jockey Cap, Hug and Silver points, old Tillamook, the singing sands, and on a sunny day that sea of cornflower blue. These had lasted.

It was time to go; one o'clock. The end of the ball, the end of the year, the end of Cannon Beach's first century. And so Mary and the rest went off, rather sadly, their evening cut so short, off to . . . where

149

ever that might be. As for the others, they went home, got into bed, turned out the lights. The fog rolled in, a little wind came up, the waves broke on the shore as they had from the beginning—and Cannon Beach went to sleep, at peace.

Appendix I

The community of Cannon Beach was incorporated in 1955, its charter enacted in 1957. In addition to a council of five members, the charter called for a strong chief executive in the person of the mayor.

In 1984 the charter was revised to provide for a city manager. The council members are elected for four-year terms on a staggered schedule.

In addition to mayor, manager, and council, there are the following bodies: Planning Commission, Design Review Board, Parks and Community Services Committee, Public Works Committee, and Energy Committee.

MAYORS:
1956: Dr. J. W. Sargent
1958: Don L. Erickson
1963: Gerald R. Gower
1975: Bruce Haskell
1979: Joe Police
1980: John Williams
1981: Lucille Houston
1987: Everett Browning
1991: Herbert Schwab
1995: Kirk Anderson

CITY MANAGERS:
1985: Mark Lindberg
1987: Del Beaver
1988: John Williams

Appendix II

The following persons were active in early attempts to found a historical society in Cannon Beach: Karolyn Adamson, David Firebaugh, Robert Gilmore, Frank Lackaff, Robert McConnell, Gainor Minott, Don Osborne, Jr., Bridget Snow, Kenneth Clark, Pat Friedland, Lucille Houston, Sandra Larson, Mae McCoy, Michael Morgan, Janet Rekate, and Margaret Sroufe.

The first board of the present society were George Shields (president), Roland Burrows, Alma and David English, David Pastor, Barbara Schwab, Ann Smeaton, Karolyn Adamson, Jim Dennon, Ron Gluth, Kent Price, Molly and Dan Schausten, and Marlene Laws. Yuri Nakata and Tim Lindsey were helpful advisers.

The present board of the Cannon Beach Historical Society are Frank Chown (president), Eleanor Chown, Roger Evanson, William Gittelsohn, Katy Grant-Hanson, Treva Haskell, Marlene Laws, Barbara Levine, Sally Little, Barbara and Herb Schwab, Ann Smeaton, and Ann Wierum.

The Society was organized for the purpose of preserving the history of Cannon Beach by seeking, collecting, and protecting historical memorabilia of all kinds, by recording oral histories, by making these materials available to the public whenever possible, and by working toward acquiring a museum for storing and displaying such materials.

The Society's holdings include oral histories on audio and video tapes, photographs, newspaper files and clippings, periodicals, manuscripts, and artifacts.

The Society is headquartered at History House, Spruce and Sunset streets, Cannon Beach. Telephone: 436-9301.

Sources

General

Dennon, James. *Cannon Beach History before 1960.* N.p., n.d.

Miller, Emma Gene. *Clatsop County, Oregon.* Binfords & Mort, 1958.

Collections of the Cannon Beach Historical Society.

Newspaper Files

The Daily Astorian

Astoria Evening Budget

The Oregonian

The Cannon

Seaside Signal

The Cannon Beach Gazette

Chapter I

Loy, William G. *Atlas of Oregon.* Eugene: University of Oregon, 1976.

Alt, David D. *Roadside Geology of Oregon.* Missoula: Mountain Press Publications, 1978.

Suttles, Wayne, ed. *Handbook of North American Indians.* Vol. 7, *Northwest Coast.* Washington, D.C.: Smithsonian Institution, 1990.

O'Donnell, Terence. *That Balance So Rare: The Story of Oregon.* *Portland*: Oregon Historical Society Press, 1988.

Moulton, Gary E., ed. *The Journals of the Lewis & Clark Expedition.* Vol. 6, Lincoln: University of Nebraska Press, 1990.

Jones, Edward Gardner, ed. *The Oregonian Handbook of the Pacific Northwest.* *Portland*: The Oregonian Publishing Company, 1894.

Hanson, Inez Stafford. *Life on Clatsop*, N.p., n.d.

Sources (continued)

Chapter II

Cumtux, (quarterly of the Clatsop County Historical Society).
 Fall 1987.

Gillespie, G. *Tillamook Rock and Light Station.* Washington, D.C.:
 Government Printing Office, 1881.

DeFrees, Madeline. *The Light Station on Tillamook Rock.* Corvallis:
 Arrowwood Books, 1990.

Chapter III

Corning, Howard McKinley. *Dictionary of Oregon History.* Portland:
 Binfords & Mort, 1984.

Chapter IV

Oregon Historical Quarterly, vol. 5 (September 1954).

Chapter V

Walth, Brent. *Fire at Eden's Gate: Tom McCall and the Oregon Story.*
 Portland: Oregon Historical Society Press, 1994.

Beals, Herbert K. *Preliminary Development Plan, Cannon Beach,
 Oregon.* Eugene: University of Oregon, 1967.

Chapters VII and VIII

The Cannon Beach Gazette.

ILLUSTRATION LIST

155

INDEX

157